# Soul
## OF THE
# Healer

## ART & STORIES OF THE PERMANENTE JOURNAL

**Tom Janisse, MD**

**Editor-in-Chief**

TPP

**The Permanente Press**

Oakland, California • Portland, Oregon

**The Permanente Press**
Oakland, California • Portland, Oregon

The Permanente Press is owned by The Permanente Federation, LLC
Oakland, California

*Editor-in-Chief:* Tom Janisse, MD, MBA
*Managing Editor:* Merry Parker
*Senior Designer:* Lynette Leisure
*Principal Editor for Soul Section:* Max McMillen
*Director of Publishing Operations:* Amy Eakin
*Production Assistant:* Sharon Sandgren

# CONTENTS BY ARTIST / AUTHOR

# Contents by Artist / Author

# Contents by Theme for Written Pieces

# Acknowledgments

Four groups who played critical roles in making this book possible deserve special recognition: the editorial and publishing staff of *The Permanente Journal (TPJ);* the reviewers who initially accepted the written pieces for publication in the journal; the selection groups who chose the images and writing for this book; and the sponsors of *TPJ*. Meaningful and beautiful books are created through the efforts of many people.

## Editorial and Publishing Staff

The editorial and publishing staff demonstrate a remarkable commitment to *The Permanente Journal* and extended their efforts to make this book a reality. Their pride in their work and the organization drives their dedication.

Lynette Leisure's vision and artistry created the worthy canvas upon which you view these works of art.

Merry Parker's guidance and shepherding have been the stable backbone in preserving our integrity and in keeping us on task.

Max McMillen's gentle editing has coaxed the authors through the sometimes frightening experience of publishing.

Amy Eakin's determination that we operate within our budget and expertise in circulation ensures that our work does not go unseen.

Sharon Sandgren, through diligence and resourcefulness, doggedly tracked every contributor to seek permissions, photographs, and biographies.

## Reviewers

Since the publication of the first issue of *The Permanente Journal,* two groups have reviewed, with thought and care, the Soul of the Healer submissions to *TPJ*. They have freely given their time, their expertise, and their compassion to those who have taken the risk to share their written works with strangers.

Initial group: Chuck Clemons, MD; Eric Schuman, PA; David Scott, MD; Kelly Sievers, CRNA; and Michael Stine, MS.

Current group: Kitty Evers, MD; Vincent Felitti, MD; Terry Laskiewicz, MD; Kelly Sievers, CRNA; and Calvin Weisberger, MD.

## Selection Groups

Two groups gave their time, energy and insight to the difficult task of choosing the images and written pieces included. I participated in both groups.

Images: Kitty Evers, MD; Terry Laskiewicz, MD; Lynette Leisure; Stu Levy, MD; and Merry Parker.

Writing: Kitty Evers, MD; Arthur Hayward, MD; Max McMillen; Kate Scannell, MD; Kelly Sievers, CRNA; and Jon Stewart.

## Sponsors

Finally, *The Permanente Journal* Editorial Team and Advisory Board acknowledge the continued significant support—both monetary and intrinsic—of the Executive Medical Directors of the Permanente Medical Groups. Ten years ago they took a chance on publishing a different sort of medical journal—this book is one of the outcomes. ❖

— Tom Janisse, MD
Editor-in-Chief

THE STORIES PEOPLE TELL
HAVE A WAY OF TAKING CARE OF THEM.
IF STORIES COME TO YOU, CARE FOR THEM.
AND LEARN TO GIVE THEM AWAY
WHERE THEY ARE NEEDED.
SOMETIMES A PERSON NEEDS A STORY
MORE THAN FOOD TO STAY ALIVE.
THAT IS WHY WE PUT THESE STORIES
IN EACH OTHER'S MEMORY.
THIS IS HOW PEOPLE
CARE FOR THEMSELVES.

— BARRY LOPEZ, AN OREGON NATURALIST,
FROM HIS NATIVE AMERICAN TALE, *CROW AND WEASEL*
SAN FRANCISCO: NORTH POINT PRESS, 1990.

# INTRODUCTION

Changing health systems, progression of chronic disease, technologic advances, and greater patient expectations make practicing medicine today an arduous task. It takes heart to turn routine interactions with patients, colleagues, and teammates into meaningful moments. It takes spirit to look forward to long days helping some patients and hoping to help others. Physicians and nurses are not just machines on a marathon schedule that require regular maintenance; they are humans that seek a source of energy and renewal. Dr. Kitty Evers, painter and poet, says, "To paint and to write is my great joy." Dr. Wuhao (Taki) Tu, our second cover artist, says "My paintings are simply my way of reacting to the beauties of the lights and the colors of nature." In line drawings, Dr. Evany Zirul delightfully portrays perceptions of people useful in understanding physical behavior. She says, "My art is figurative. It is realism expressing the maleness, femaleness, and emotional nuances mirrored by our bodies." Several of our artists and authors are retired. After completing clinical practice they continue to enrich their lives through art.

## Why This Book?

Inspired by our readers' comments and high rating of the "Soul of Healer" section of *The Permanente Journal (TPJ)*, we created this book to bring together the art and stories they remark are so beautiful and uplifting. This *Soul of the Healer* book is organized chronologically from the first issue in Summer 1997 to the Fall 2003 issue. Selected pieces are grouped together by issue. Contributors' biographies accompany their work, so you get to know them and hear their voices. The written pieces have also been indexed in the Table of Contents by theme. I want to especially thank those artists and authors who took a chance on a new publication and submitted their work for the early issues.

## Artists and Authors

The 41 visual artists and 22 authors that populate this book with their creations exemplify the soul of Permanente. Presenting their pieces here gives durability to the meaning and enjoyment they create. The effect will linger for physicians and nurses new in practice, established in practice, and longer in practice to rediscover meaning in medicine.

## Art and Medicine

Several artists have noted in their profiles that a strong relationship exists between art and medicine. Dr. Mohamed Osman, whose Web site is rated by Google® as number one in the world for the category of contemporary African art, is a self-taught artist, and credits his medical knowledge with enhancing his art. Dr. Tina M Smith, a plastic surgeon, says, "I love the creative process in many mediums, but plastic surgery is where the culmination of my disparate interests and talents allow their best and most important expression." Dr. David Bovill notes that "Each of my sculptures represents a patient or colleague. These sculptures help me remember that I am treating people, not simply bones, joints, or x-rays." Dr. Roland Tcheng explains that "Photography appeals to me for the same reasons I enjoy medicine. There is a science and an art component to both. One can master the science and technicalities of controlling the camera, lens, and film, but without interacting with the subject and light in a personal, human way, the photographer will fail. The same can be said for succeeding in medicine and helping patients. In addition, photography forces me to look more carefully, to see more clearly, to search for patterns and contrasting elements … all of which I practice every time I examine a patient." And, Don Wissusik, says, "I have always challenged myself to take a blank piece of paper and use it to express emotions and feelings that are not easy to place into words."

In addition, these artists and authors experience a deep engagement and participation in the natural environment. They then express this in images or words. For example, about the experience of photographing a golden aspen grove at the base of the Teton Mountains at cloud break, Dr. Richard Mittleman said, "This image is magical. The experience was religious."

## Why Write? Why Paint?

Why do doctors and nurses write stories? And why tell them to a group of unfamiliar colleagues around a table? People write and paint to learn from their experiences, to express the meaning of their life's work, and to enjoy the world. Although we remember our stories, it's only when we tell them out loud or write our stories on paper, moving them out into the world, that we understand them. Barry Lopez, an Oregon naturalist, wrote in his Native American tale, *Crow and Weasel*, "The stories people tell have a way of taking care of them. If stories come to you, care for them. And learn to give them away where they are needed. Sometimes a person needs a story more than food to stay alive. That is why we put these stories in each other's memory. This is how people care for themselves."[1]

### Relevance of Writing

Reading and writing stories of clinical encounters with patients or colleagues can improve the diagnostic and communication components of physicians' and nurses' clinical competence.[2] Physicians and nurses encounter many dilemmas in their practice: moral, ethical, legal, social, human rights, religious, economic, and personal values. Stories help us understand and find solutions. Stories integrate and organize complicated situations, and so clear the mind. Writing can also positively impact physician health.[3]

Dr. Kate Scannell, author of "The Death of the Good Doctor," and keynote speaker at the *TPJ* Narrative Medicine writing workshops, wrote in *Annals of Internal Medicine*, "Writing and speaking about doctoring can save your life. By this I do not mean that they can prolong life, but, rather, that they can prove deeply enlivening. Giving language to what we witness lifts into personal and, sometimes, public consciousness the otherwise unarticulated existential dimensions of experience that permeate our work— whether we name them or not. Consciously narrating these accounts illuminates more of our collective lives as patients and physicians, expanding our felt understanding of human frailty, compassion, strength, love, fear, hatred, and ill will."[4]

### Writing Groups

*TPJ* has conducted writing conferences and workshops and now sponsors two writing groups, one in Portland, Oregon, and the second in Oakland, California, to bring doctors and nurses together to read and receive comment on their work, and to foster the healing power of a group supporting and sharing with each other. Physicians participate in other groups. From these forums they send writing to *TPJ*. Dr. Mark Katz notes in his profile, "This piece was written for my creative nonfiction writing group, which has met biweekly since 1997." Dr. John J Kuiper, says, "Upon completion of a drawing class, I rendered this 16"x20" graphite drawing of medical equipment that, with the exception of the newer stethoscope, served me for 43 years."

### Enjoy Your Journey

Ultimately, we hope that as you page through this book, pausing to reflect on the beautiful images and reading the poems and stories, your journey is enriched. ❖

— Tom Janisse, MD
Editor-in-Chief

References

1. Lopez B. Crow and weasel. San Francisco: North Point Press, 1990.
2. Charon R. Welcome and Introduction. Presented at Narrative Medicine: A Colloquium. 2003 May 2-3. Columbia University. New York, New York.
3. Pennebaker JW. Opening up: The healing power of expressing emotions. New York: The Guilford Press, 1990.
4. Scannell K. Writing for our lives: Physician narratives and medical practice. Ann Intern Med 2002 Nov;137(9):779-81.

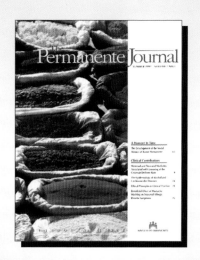

The Permanente Journal
SUMMER 1997 · VOLUME 1 · NO. 1

**SUMMER 1997**

*be healer*

**Pigments**
photograph
Pictured are face and body
pigments for sale outside
an ancient Hindu temple
on the Bagmati River near
Kathmandu, Nepal.

**David Clarke, MD,** is a
gastroenterologist for
Northwest Permanente in
Clackamas, OR. The walls
of Dr. Clarke's home are
littered with photographs
taken during his travels.

*soul of t*

## Losin' Control of the Reins
### *(song lyrics)*

He used to sit tall in the saddle.
Now he sits in an old rockin' chair.
While the kids fight a cowboy and Indian battle,
Grandpa just sits and stares.
He used to ride 'em and rope 'em.
He could wrestle a steer with his hands.
Now the doc says, "No drinkin' or smokin'.
Better get all the rest that you can."

He's losin' control of the reins,
Saddled with old aches and pains.
I wish that you could have seen him back when
Cowboys all called him a man among men.
No horse was too tough to tame.
Times were rough, but he'd never complain.
And now faded memories are all that remain.
He's losin' control of the reins.

This mornin', we all sat in silence
When the doc came to see him again.
He said, "His heart's given out.
Your pa's livin' out his last days.
I just can't tell you when."
Now he sits on the porch in the twilight.
He pats his old dog on the head.
And I say, "Daddy, it's night time.
I guess it's high time
We get this old cowboy to bed."

He's losin' control of the reins,
Saddled with old aches and pains.
I wish that you could have seen him back when
Cowboys all called him a man among men.
No horse was too tough to tame.
Times were rough, but he'd never complain.
And now faded memories are all that remain.
He's losin' control of the reins.

It's natural, I know
But it's sad just the same to see him
Losin' control of the reins.

**Arthur Schlosser, MD, aka Dean Dobbins,** is a pediatrician for the Southern California Permanente Medical Group in Panorama City. He is also a country music singer/songwriter who goes by the name Dean Dobbins. Visit his Web page at www.newenterprises.com/dobbins.

# Evany Zirul, MFA, DO

My art is figurative.
It is realism expressing
the maleness, femaleness
and emotional nuances
mirrored by our bodies.

**My Attitude to Smoking**
line art

**Visit to the Nursing Home**
line art

Evany Zirul, MFA, DO, formerly an ear,
nose, throat and facial plastic surgeon
for the Permanente Medical Group of
Mid-America in Kansas City, MO, creates line
drawings and bronze sculptures.

## They All Know

We call it somewhat crassly "peek and shriek." Each of us who has had the privilege of opening the body's cavities has, at some time or other, sooner or later, been victim of the foul surprise: cancer everywhere and nothing to do about it. The shriek is a silent one, more of an "oh shit" sans exclamation mark than a cry of terror; it is for the other, the patient, that those too-numerous-to-count, hard white blobs of flesh hold significance: the significance of one's mortality, all bold and ready, all cold and patient and waiting; but not for long. We spend time treading water, pushing aside loop after loop of intestine swollen by the cruel, malignant trick, delaying the inevitable decision to close the incision and quietly retreat. The room falls silent. Some comment is made regarding the patient's age: "how terrible" if young, "well, at least he's eighty" if old, as if the accumulation of years justifies the insult of death.

One or another of the operating team promises to get that colonoscopy at an early age, or the long-delayed mammogram in the hope of forestalling their own "peek and shriek" some years hence. Each turns inwardly to the thought of those loving and loved; gratitude mixes with the gravity of the moment, and we each celebrate our aliveness, our seeming wholeness. As the minutes slip by and the case draws to its close, I rehearse my speech in silence. I curse the job that at times brings me such joy, at other times such agonizing moments as these, moments for which no Jordan-esque salary would be enough. I usually stay until the bitter end, often applying the dressing, half to delay the coming conversation, half to reconcile my impotence with the reality of the magnitude of my foe.

> IN THAT INSTANT I CAN ONLY WISH THAT I HAD CHOSEN A PROFESSION WHERE FAILURE IS MET IN SOME OTHER WAY; WHERE INABILITY DIDN'T COST A LIFE.

Finally it's over, and I rip my gown and gloves away, thanking my team who scurry about, cleaning the gore I've left behind; cleansing the room to cleanse their souls, moving quickly to the next, almost certainly happier case. I huddle with the chart and telephone, writing and dictating the mundanities that make up the medical record, a document which, for all its sterile language remains the most consistently dramatic of all written testimonies: the story of the beginning of a death.

I can delay it no more. A fifty-foot walk becomes a morose marathon as my brain buzzes to create the patina of professionalism: the firm confidence and quiet reassuring that I alone know are platitudes, but to his family are the threads of hope in a life's fabric come unwoven. I'll never get over how stupidly I always begin these reports. The half smile I wear can fool no one, but I can't make it go away. "Everything went well; he's fine," I always begin. The complete and bald lie that "he's fine" is unbetrayed by my tone in those first words. Their eyes flash for a moment, hands clutching arms, and the first tears, those of relief begin to swell in their eyes.

"But I'm afraid . . ." Afraid? Afraid of what? What a silly figure of speech! My fear is the reality of mortality. What is that fear compared to theirs when I finish my sentence, ". . . the news isn't good." In that instant I can only wish that I had chosen a profession where failure is met in some other way; where inability didn't cost a life. I usually just wish I were high on Haleakala's shoulders, breathing the thin, cold air that blows so hard across the home of my God. The arm clutched in reassurance seconds ago is released to its own devices as almost every hand reaches to cover a mouth opened in a gasp, a gasp of angry disbelief, and bitter anguish. The description of the findings follows, euphemized, painted in pastel instead of blood, purposely sanitized by my jargon to leave that glimmer of hope where I know only hopelessness is real. They always say, "But you took it out, didn't you?" as if the cancer were a weed to be pulled. It's words I stumble over yet again as I try to explain the futility of "getting it out." I wish they could see the cancer: the countless tumors that everywhere bulge and glisten, almost smiling as they cover the surface of his guts. I want them to know in their hearts as I do that it simply can't be done, that I can't "get it all."

I rely on my time-tested deception: "It would kill him to take it all out," I say with a set jaw and a straight face, knowing full well that it's a lie, but also knowing that these words seem to convey the truth—that we have met our match. I offer them reassurances, retreating to the safety of statistics to leave that glimmer of hope that I know doesn't exist but believe must never be extinguished. We briefly discuss further treatment, me knowing it won't work, them certain it will. And then, with little more, it's over.

We both don't want it to end. I feel better having broken the news, having finished the first dreaded task.

> THE PATIENT USES THE TIME TO STRUGGLE FOR CONSCIOUSNESS, REAWAKENING IN A WORLD OF BLINDING PAIN, COLD AND HARSH LIGHT. I USE THE TIME TO COLLECT MYSELF, REMEMBERING THAT THE TASK OF INFORMING THE PATIENT WILL BE MINE AS WELL.

They are comforted by my presence, by the gaudy green of my scrubs, by the bleached white of my coat, and by the ever-increasing streaks of gray in my hair. I don't pretend to understand why this is so, but I've felt it time and again: their silently asking me to stay, as if I'll change my mind, change my story, change the truth. I'll often bend to hug his wife, or place my left hand on her husband's shoulder as I shake his right. "I'll take good care of him," I vow, as if that will somehow make everything all right, as if I can make up for the failing. I turn to take on the morose marathon in reverse; it's only slightly easier in this direction. I always see them in the corner of my eye as I return to the sanctuary of my operating room. Always they're sobbing, hugging, and sobbing. I always sigh, as if this deep breath will clear my heart as well as my lungs, and with a shake of my head close the door behind me.

Recovery from anesthesia works in two directions in these cases. The patient uses the time to struggle for consciousness, reawakening in a world of blinding pain, cold and harsh light. I use the time to collect myself, remembering that the task of informing the patient will be mine as well. With luck, the case is late in the day. The patient retires to the bliss that is morphine. I retire to the laughter of my children, the arms of my wife, and a deep, forgetful sleep.

The next morning again brings pain. Post-op day one is a blizzard of nausea and morphine to the man who hours ago stood smiling and confident, joking with me that he felt lucky to have a young surgeon, as I must still remember what they taught me.

His wife is at the bedside as I make my rounds. She's holding his hand as if this were his deathbed, scarcely concealing her terror at being left alone after thirty years of marriage. He is, thankfully, comfortably numb. The narcotics are working their subtle magic. I walk in, erect and seemingly proud, extending my hand in greeting, not noticing that it is shaking. "Good morning. You did good yesterday," is the attempt at a pleasant greeting. His eyes appear sunken, the pupils tiny black dots in a sea of green.

"So how d'ya do, doc?" he asks, wincing with the effort. It becomes clear that she has told him nothing of our conversation yesterday. She's embarrassed by this, of course, but I've come to expect little else. "I did fine and so did you," I reply, clearly dodging the point.

"Did ya get it all?" he asks with a wink.

"Well I'm afraid . . ." there's that 'afraid' again, as if I had something to fear. " . . . it's pretty bad." I curse the God that gave me this language, this job, this inability to forestall mortality. I want so many better words. But the patient will have none of it.

"Hey, you did the best you could." He dismisses me with a wave of his hand. And I, me, the surgeon, the healer, the doctor, quickly accept this endorsement; accept it because it comforts me, because it forgives me.

"Yes, I did," I mutter somewhat obsequiously. I beat a hasty retreat. Sometime later that day, I pass by his room again. He's brushing his teeth despite the fact that he's attached to two towers of equipment and tubes; brushing his teeth because it gives him the dignity of being human in this place where dignity and modesty are the earliest casualties.

I come upon him as he's seated in front of the mirror, comfortable in his morphine-induced euphoria. "You knew, didn't you?" I asked, safe in the knowledge that years in this business will give.

"Yeah, I guess I did," he replies without a trace of regret.

"How long have you been sick?" I ask, hoping that his self-induced delay will somehow clear me of all guilt in the matter.

"A while," he says, still brushing.

"Why didn't you come in sooner?" I said.

"I just knew it was my time, and I didn't want to worry Phyllis," he offers unapologetically. I touch him on the shoulder, feeling the strength that wells up inside of him.

"Thanks doc," he says.

"For what," I reply in surprise, "I didn't do anything."

"You told her," he says, "I couldn't."

"So you knew."

"Yeah, I knew."

He knew. They all know. By God, they all just know. ❖

**Thomas Paluch, MD,** is a general surgeon for the Southern California Permanente Medical Group, specializing in minimally invasive surgery. He lives in a 112-year-old house in San Diego with his wife and two children. With some friends from Kaiser Permanente, he has ridden Race Across America, a cross-country bicycle race, twice, and has won the corporate division. When he's not riding or operating, he enjoys playing blues guitar.

The
Permanente Journal

FALL 1997    VOLUME 1 NO. 2

FALL 1997

*soul of t.*

**El Capitan**
watercolor

MY PAINTINGS
ARE SIMPLY
MY WAY OF
REACTING TO
THE BEAUTIES OF
THE LIGHTS
AND THE COLORS
OF NATURE.

**Wuhao (Taki) Tu, MD,** is a retired nephrologist-internist. He worked for The Permanente Medical Group from 1962-1988. To see more of his artwork, visit his Web site at www.takitu.com.

## A Father's Ritual

standing on tip toes
my chin rests on the anvil shoulders
of my teenage son

this son who once straddled *my* shoulders asks
"Now what, Dad?"

we review again
the lesson on
tying the necktie

I watch
our reflection
as the sacred rite unfolds

like the cascading mirrors
of the barber shop
before and behind

I see my father's fathers
and my son's sons
looping the colored cloth

tying the yolk

as he gets ready for work

**Edmund Shaheen, MD,** joined the
Southern California Permanente Medical
Group in Woodland Hills in 1976. He is a
family practitioner and a physician
acupuncturist, working on his master's
degree in Chinese Medicine. Dr. Shaheen
enjoys foreign languages, anthropology,
blues harmonica, and the musical saw.

**Visit to the Plastic Surgeon**
line art

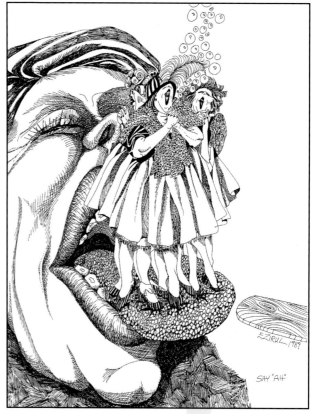

**Say Ah**
line art

More information about
**Evany Zirul, MFA, DO,**
can be found on page 4.

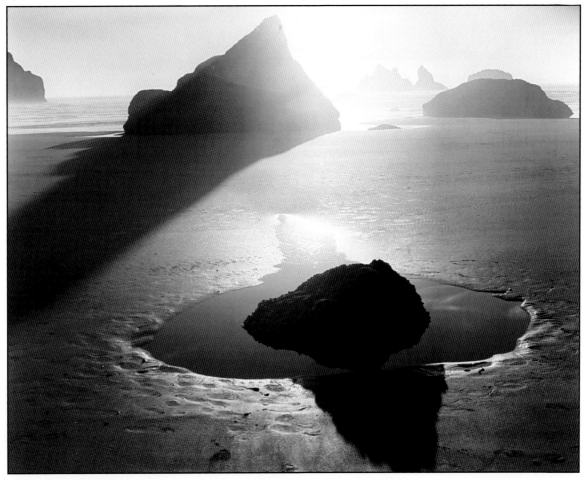

**Bandon Beach, Oregon**

photograph

**Stu Levy, MD,** is a family practice physician for Northwest Permanente in Vancouver, WA. He studied photography with Ansel Adams and has taught many photography workshops. Dr. Levy has shown his work at over 20 one-person shows. His photographs are in several major collections, including the Portland Art Museum, the Portland Visual Chronicle, and the Center for Creative Photography in Tucson, AZ.

## Epic Encounter

i TRIED to let them
reprogram my brain;

sit quietly,
click appropriately,
enter data only
when prompted.

But my body,
my body kept
jumping out of the chair,
pacing,
stretching,
distracting,
intervening.

At first I blamed the caffeine,
poor sleep, bad posture, or karma.

But soon I was aware there
is this struggle—
so I used the pen;
at least I can
fight a small battle
on familiar turf
and win;

Before the defensive positions
of my cyberspace
(never knew I had one)
are completely overrun.

**Milton Tepper Cohen, MD,** has been practicing primary care medicine for 23 years. He works for Northwest Permanente in Clackamas, OR.

**Joe Oleniacz, MD,** was a pediatrician for The Carolina Permanente Medical Group, until joining Chapel Hill Pediatrics in 1999. He is married and has two children.

## Managing Chaos

Always ask, "what else?"
pan for hidden gold.
Expect the worst,
listen to that inner voice
where Nature hides her doom.
When things are good,
never brag
lest wanting blame for bad.
When behind, slow down,
dot that i, recheck that lab.
When angry, smile.
Ruffled, sit.
Hurried, pause.
Give ten when asked for one.
Listen.
Smile.
Shake that hand.
Touch.
Touch.
Touch again.
And foremost, do no harm.
What else?

**J Trig Brown, MD, MPH,** was a general
internist with The Carolina Permanente
Medical Group, and Chief of Internal
Medicine for Durham and Chapel Hill.
He is now with Durham Internal Medicine.

WINTER 1998

*soul of t*

**Sunset Reflection, Buda Castle, Budapest**

photograph

**Punchbowl Falls, Oregon**

photograph

More information about
**Stu Levy, MD,** can be
found on page 12.

**Toupees by Al**
line art

**Select-a-Nose**
line art

See page 4 for more information
about **Evany Zirul, MFA, DO.**

*soul of t*

SPRING 1998

*he healer*

# JANET NEUBURG, MD

MY FAMILY
HAS A STRONG
PHOTOGRAPHY
HERITAGE ...

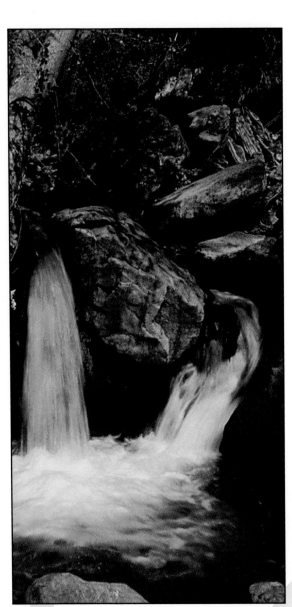

**Deer Creek, Grand
Canyon, Arizona**
photograph

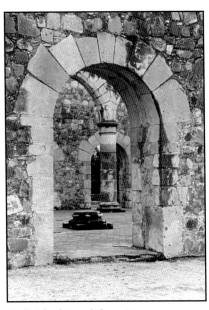

**Unfinished Dominican Monastery**
photograph
A monastery built in the 1700s,
Culiapan, Oaxaca, Mexico.

**Janet Neuburg, MD,** is a physician in Occupational
Health for Northwest Permanente. Her family has a strong
photography heritage, which includes her interest in the
art of photography beginning at 15 years of age.

**Vase of Flowers**
line art

**Vase with Plant**
line art

**Stephen Bachhuber, MD,** is an anesthesiologist for Northwest Permanente in Clackamas, OR.

## Mark Katz, MD

# Earning A Second Doughnut

I'll never forget the moment I saved a doctor's life.

He was—and still is—a doctor of optometry, not a medical doctor, but a human on God's earth all the same. Sixty-four-year-old Ralph Peters entered the ER early one Tuesday morning with his wife at his side, his face ashen as he complained of severe chest pain. He didn't know it then, but he was about to develop the fatal rhythm disturbance known as ventricular fibrillation.

It was around 5:30 am, and it was my usual Monday overnight shift. I was especially rosy this morning—I had slept until 4:30 am in the call room as it had been quiet and the other two doctors on duty didn't need to call me until then. I had already downed a cup of coffee—a fresh brew that I had prepared myself. My teeth were freshly brushed and my mouth rinsed generously with cinnamon-flavored Viadent.

The major anxiety on my mind at the moment I saw Dr. Peters walk through the door with his fist over his chest—an interesting gesture which signifies surrender and/or angina pectoris—was that the department had become rather busy in the previous 15 to 30 minutes. The early morning hours of 4 to 8 am are known medically for a higher incidence of heart attacks, but, in addition, these hours often herald a parade of patients who need work excuses for the preceding day they have just missed—often feigned as "a cold which I just got over yesterday."

"Paul," I said to the other doctor in the department, "If you can see the rash in room 2, the UTI in 3, and start on the abdominal pain in 7, who looks stable, I'll get to this chest pain." Indeed, in ways more than metaphysical, in the lingua franca of emergency medicine, patients became and indeed were their diseases.

"My pleasure, Mark," he smiled, his kindness sincere! He was a cardiology fellow who was moonlighting with us, and it always felt reassuring to have a cardiologist on hand when the vapors smacked of something serious about to happen.

I erased the "TBS" ("to be seen") notation next to the name "Peters" which had been placed on the huge white traffic board and placed my "MK." I entered the room, noticing that my pens were lined up neatly in my pocket and that there were no stains on my new white coat. The patient was taking off his maroon LaCoste shirt and had sat down on the hospital cart.

"Hello, Mr. Peters, I'm Dr. Katz, the emergency physician on—"

"*Doctor* Peters," emphasized his wife, who was hastily dressed but with time nevertheless for lipstick. It seemed more important to her than to him, and he just smiled. Lynn, the nurse, placed oxygen prongs into her patient's nostrils as his wife spoke.

"Oh, excuse me, Doctor Peters," I politely corrected myself.

Now, at that moment, many of my fellow emergency physicians would have declared war, albeit a tacit war. The offense would be to use terms so technical and grandiose as to leave the enemy tethered and begging for mercy in the form of: "Could you please explain that to me? I don't understand."

But as for me, I was feeling centered as the caffeine coursed through my blood and thus inquired: "Oh, what kind of doctor are you? This helps me to know how technically to explain things."

"I'm an optometrist," he smiled again, as I noted the scratch on my eyeglasses and how spotless his were. He appeared to be in less pain since the oxygen had been started and he had been placed at rest.

I quickly set out to obtain a history while Lynn placed cardiac monitor leads on Dr. Peters' chest. His wife stood close by in this 8-by-10 foot treatment room; I was used to feeling claustrophobic, but I have always felt that a patient in an emergency department who so desires should be allowed at least one friend or family member present.

He told me as his wife stood by silently that he had developed the crushing chest pain 45 minutes earlier, during sexual intercourse (at which time I wondered if his wife's lipstick was applied before, during, or after; and I silently congratulated this couple on being sexually active at 4:30 am!), that he had never had chest pain before, and that he and his wife were both CPR instructors. Thus, they knew this could be a heart attack. The chest pain was still present but was mild compared with the peak around 30 minutes earlier. I ordered a nitroglycerin tablet, and, as it dissolved under his tongue, I looked into his eyes and realized he was frightened.

I had already determined from his history that he would be "a keeper"—even if this were stomach gas or a pulled muscle, new chest pain in a man over age 50 gets the so-called "full court press."

"It's irregular," his wife nervously pointed out, and I observed, as I glanced at her now, much greater concern for her husband's heartbeat than even for his professional title. I looked up, my index finger on Ralph's radial pulse, and saw clear evidence of premature ventricular contractions.

We needed an IV line immediately in order to give a dose of lidocaine. I might have appeared calm to someone who didn't know me well, but I also knew my right leg was shaking uncontrollably under the white coat. Lynn was occupied with the EKG, which was also key at this moment to help diagnose a possible heart attack.

I walked out of the room, and another nurse, Steve, stood nearby drawing up an antibiotic I had ordered for a man in the next room who had been diagnosed with strep throat.

"Steve, I need you right now, please, to start an IV, stat, right here in 11. He's got multifocals with chest pain." I was simultaneously gentle and firm.

He clearly heard me and, competent nurse that he was, placed the line within a single minute. As the line was taped in place, I saw multiple PVCs again on the monitor, so frequent now that I assumed Dr. Peters would be dizzy or having some symptoms therefrom.

With my hand on his pulse, my eyes looking over at the computer-read EKG that Lynn was pulling out of the machine that read, "Acute myocardial infarction," I asked him, "Are you dizzy at all?"

"Nope," he smiled, "and I feel real confident in you. What's up?"

"Well, it appears you're in the earliest stages of a heart attack," and I returned the compliment by smiling and speaking calmly. "And you're certainly in the right place, because we can take care of anything which happens from this moment on." (Not entirely true, but there are moments when reassuring the patient becomes tantamount to the realities which may supervene.)

"Lynn, give Dr. Peters an aspirin to chew,

> As my shift ended,
> I performed my usual
> Tuesday morning
> ritual ... stopping
> at Yum Yum on the
> next block for a
> chocolate-covered,
> old-fashioned
> doughnut.

stat, and draw up 100 of lidocaine. Also start a drip at 2 per minute, and I'd like a half-bolus—"

I cut my own words off as I saw the monitor above my head, but behind his, change its wave form to the entirely irregular saw-tooth form which could only mean one thing.

"Call a Code!" I shouted out to Michelle, seated ten yards away at the clerk's desk. I quickly and methodically rattled off orders as if delivering my lines in a play I had acted in every night for several years: Lay him flat! Oxygenate him with the Ambu bag! Get the crash cart over here! Start CPR! Get ready to defibrillate super-stat!

I recited my part, but I felt my mouth become sticky as cotton as his eyes rolled back and his face became plethoric. He began to froth at the mouth as his limbs contorted into spasms followed by seizure-like waves.

"Where's that defibrillator?" I snapped to Steve, who appeared with the huge red, oversized tool-box-like contraption within another ten seconds.

I turned around to see that Mrs. Peters was gone and in her place stood two nurses and a respiratory therapist who had come to assist with the resuscitation. I began performing CPR on the chest of this CPR instructor who was probably in the bliss of orgasm an hour ago and was now in the process of actively dying.

"Bag him, please, Gina," I ordered the respiratory therapist until he could be properly intubated by the anesthesiologist.

The moments of waiting for the defibrillator seemed like hours, and I imagined Mrs. Peters calling her lawyer and reporting, "He came in walking and talking. They didn't start the IV soon enough. I even saw the PVCs. They've killed him!"

As I compressed Ralph Peters' sternum the requisite 1.5 to 2 inches mandated by the American Heart Association, I looked at his lifeless face, and I felt some of the life drain from mine.

Within the next minute, the paddles were placed on his chest by the charge nurse, Liz. "Shock him at 200," I proclaimed, and I heard the combination zip-hum of the machine as it warmed up, and with a touch of the red button, its accumulated wattage surged through Dr. Peters' chest.

Within three seconds, the monitor showed evidence of restoring a normal heart rhythm.

I breathed more easily as he began to breathe on his own—still with the assistance of oxygen, but his diaphragm was now spontaneously contracting as it had done approximately 10 million times a year since his birth.

Mrs. Peters now appeared in the doorway and, with a lump in her throat, asked, "Is he back?"

I looked down at her husband, whose eyes were now opening as he put his hands almost reflexively to his chest, to the site where the current had entered.

"You're okay now, Dr. Peters. Your heart went into a faulty rhythm, but we've corrected it and have the situation well in hand."

"He's doing okay now," I said to Mrs. Peters. "Would you like to come in?" I offered. I realized as she stepped into the room that for the more than 500 patients I had taken care of in cardiac arrest over my 19 years as an emergency physician, all but a few were in arrest at the time I first came upon them. It was easy to objectify and depersonify someone with whom you never have had a conversation. But to see someone to whom you have been speaking suddenly "go out"—this causes the heart of the nonfibrillating onlooker to palpitate furiously!

As if to rescue me from my probably visible anxiety, Ralph began to speak, his words directed at me. "It was a dream. I saw you and everyone else in black and white, moving without words and in slow motion, almost like the blacklights we used to have. Then you all suddenly came to in color again and I heard voices—'he's back,' or something like that."

His wife took his hand, and, as she squeezed it, she said "I love you" to him and "Thank you" to me, in such rapid succession, that the combination caused my eyes to engorge with tears. "You saved his life, Dr. Katz," she acknowledged.

"We actually had the entire staff here to act swiftly," I said. "It's our job, and we're glad you came in when you did."

I accompanied Ralph and his wife in the elevator to the intensive care unit, feeling as if I was bouncing on the same high-pressure oxygen that we had given him a few minutes earlier. I said "Good morning" to people I would have usually merely nodded to.

As my shift ended, I performed my usual Tuesday morning ritual of driving away from the Kaiser Permanente campus and stopping at Yum Yum on the next block for a chocolate-covered, old-fashioned doughnut.

As a counterboy in my Dad's luncheonette 35 years earlier, I used to wonder how people could eat the same thing every morning, but now, on the other side of the counter, I found a sense of security in the consistency of my request! I often thought about the calories, empty ones at that, contained in these beautifully shiny glazed confections, which nevertheless afforded me some sense of tranquillity that I desired, if not deserved, after my overnight shifts.

I also appreciated now that both countergirls knew my order as soon as they saw me enter. I gave Rosa a dollar tip this particular morning, then smiled and exchanged greetings as she all but bowed to me. After leaving the shop, I quickly finished the doughnut before even my first sip of coffee.

I stopped walking toward the car and felt a pang of desire—for another 450 calories—but today it didn't bother me. I turned around and retraced my steps into the shop and told a smiling Rosa, "I'll have another one, please!" ❖

**Mark Katz, MD,** joined the Southern California Permanente Medical Group in 1985. He is a hospitalist and HIV specialist in the Department of Internal Medicine in West Los Angeles and is the Physician Co-Coordinator for HIV/AIDS. This piece was written for his creative nonfiction writing group, which has met biweekly since 1997.

More information about
**Stephen Bachhuber, MD,**
can be found on page 21.

**SUMMER 1998**

*soul of t*

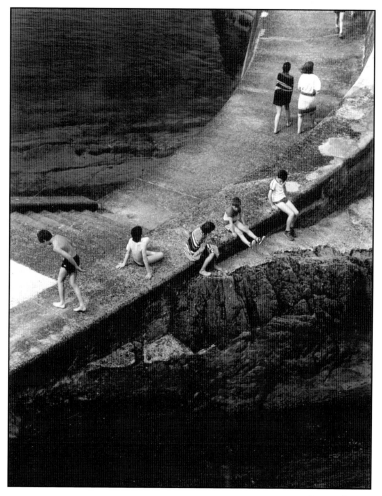

"PIER, ARDMORE" IS PART OF AN ONGOING PHOTO ESSAY OF IRELAND I HAVE BEEN WORKING ON SINCE 1982.

**Pier, Ardmore**
photograph

**Eric Blau, MD,** is a Physician-in-Charge for Preventive Medicine for the Southern California Permanente Medical Group at the San Diego Medical Center, CA. He is a long-time fine arts photographer and is a recipient of an Artist Support Grant from the Polaroid Corporation. He has published two books on photography.

## Kitty Evers, MD

## The Doctor

Able to weep for your youth

Able to weep for that sense of blessing at the first cry of new life

Able to weep for that time when you could stay up all night and still greet the new day

Able to smell the sweet green of grass

Able to see magic inside an ear

Able to weep at his story

Able to weep at her death

Able to be moved by tears and joy

Where has it all gone

Why are your pockets so empty

And where shall you go to come alive again …

**Kitty Evers, MD,** is a retired physician from Northwest Permanente in Portland, OR. She is the Medical Director of Physician's Advocate Resources and Lead Physician for the Health and Renewal Program.

**DR. GARFIELD - KAISER PHYSICIAN**

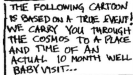

**DR. GARFIELD - PERMANENTE PHYSICIAN**

More information about
**Joe Oleniacz, MD,** can
be found on page 14.

# George Lewis, MD

To me, the most successful images are the result of finding and interpreting the abstract in the commonplace.

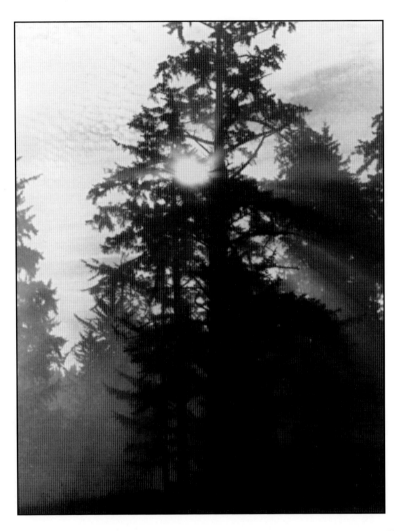

**Shore Acres**
photograph
This picture was taken during a photography workshop in Shore Acres, which is south of Coos Bay, on the Oregon Coast.

**George Lewis, MD,** is retired from Southern California Permanente Medical Group. He was a pediatrician and served as Medical Director of the Southern California Kaiser Permanente Craniofacial/Cleft Palate Team. His interest in photography goes back to his days in high school, where he worked on the yearbook. The images he produces represent his emotional response to subject matter discovered in nature as well as in man-made objects. The emotional response may be of pleasure, sadness, humor, or awe.

## Test Results, Positive

There is no magic in my bag
No aces up these white coat sleeves
No healing spells, no tricks to please
No Merlin's song to save the day.

To comfort you should be my trick
Should be our goal, our common boast.
To do no harm, my solemn oath
Is jeopardized by what I know.

The words I chant will shake your soul
Will bubble forth to change your life
Like sorcerers with beards of white
Will make you yearn for days gone by.

The news I bring is from the void.
It summons grief, directs the storms.
A crimson cape of life's dreams torn
This wizard waves before your eyes.

I mix my brew, you toss it down.
The genie's out, the truth is loose,
Your perfect health: a painful ruse.
No magic words will save you now.

More information about
**J Trig Brown, MD, MPH,**
can be found on page 15.

## A Shoulder Softly Touched

On the surface, the Triangle Hospice 5-K FunRun appears to be just another road race. At the starting line, I stand among a crowd of healthy men and women of all ages. Their brightly-colored tee shirts brag about prior conquests, a 10-K here, a marathon there. In an instant, the starting horn blares and I join the pack pounding the pavement through the streets of historic Hillsborough, North Carolina.

The course winds through old neighborhoods where spectators rock on porches, sipping their morning coffee. Many glance up from their newspapers with looks of surprise. Somewhere breakfast is served; the smell of bacon mocks our lean pack as we hurry past. A few leaves, chased by the early October breeze, flutter across our trail. We run up hills and down, eventually turning back toward the sleepy business district.

Before long, these steep hills wear me down. My legs are heavy. I sweat despite the cool morning air. With chest heaving, I struggle for breath. My gut aches as if I have run into the fist of an attacking prize fighter. My pace slows and the summit of the current hill seems fixed in the distance.

Ahead stands a group of Hospice volunteers and staff. They cheer. They coach. They energetically jump up and down. They shout words of encouragement and clap frantically for me to continue. One extends a hand holding cool water to moisten my lips. Another softly touches my shoulder as I inch past.

Their images fill my head. I see their hands bathing a dying cancer patient. I hear their soft voices whispering words of encouragement to their young patients with AIDS, telling those who are dying that they are not alone. I picture them supporting the families who ache so strongly under mountains of grief. I visualize them nurturing, comforting, calming, and caressing. They touch, soothe, and steady.

These images lift my chin, straighten my back. Their words lighten my legs and lift me over the summit. They propel me effortlessly toward the finish line. These images give me the strength to press on for those who can no longer run. ❖

More information about
**J Trig Brown, MD, MPH,**
can be found on page 15.

FALL 1998

*he healer*

IT WAS SIMPLY MY
REACTION TO THE
DANCING LIGHT
AND THE LIFE OF
THE EARLY SPRING.

**Spring**

oil

This painting was done some years ago in the moment of excitement when Dr. Tu came upon an open field of the foothill of Mount Diablo in the East Bay of Northern California.

More information about **Wuhao (Taki) Tu, MD,** can be found on page 9.

*soul of t*

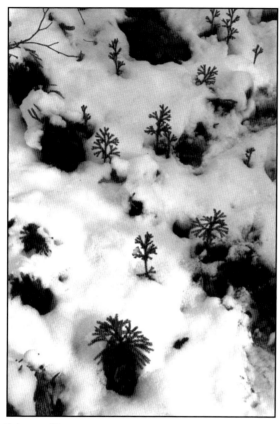

**Princess Pine**
photograph

I HAVE BEEN DRAWING AND PAINTING FOR EIGHT YEARS, AND CONTINUE TO EXPLORE THE INTERNAL EMOTIONAL LANDSCAPE AS WELL AS THE BALANCE OF BEAUTY AND CONFLICT IN THE PHYSICAL WORLD.

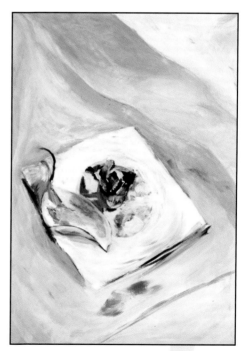

**Untitled**
acrylic

**Terry Laskiewicz, MD,** is a Board-certified internist and has worked in the internal medicine and trauma clinic for Northwest Permanente in Clackamas, OR since 1988.

WINTER 1999

*soul of t*

**Hope**
acrylic

See page 35 for more
information about
**Terry Laskiewicz, MD.**

**Young girl, handcuffs, springtime, and silver dollars**
acrylic

**Leaving Home**
acrylic

See page 35 for more information about **Terry Laskiewicz, MD.**

*soul of t*

RENATE G JUSTIN, MD

# The Exception to a Rule

"The natural anxiety, the solitude which the physician experiences at the sickness of a wife, a child, or anyone who by ties of consanguinity is rendered peculiarly dear to him, tend to obscure his judgment, and produce timidity and irresolution in his practice."[1]

"You'll assist, won't you?" the surgeon, with whom I had worked for years, asked me. Well ... yes ..., I assisted with all my patients who needed surgery, but this time? In my own practice, I had witnessed the tragic consequences of physicians treating members of their family. The wife of an orthopedist came to see me with extensive hair loss, looking like a blimp. She had every other known side effect of prolonged use of high-dose cortisone, which had been supplied to her from her husband's sample closet to treat her severe asthma.

A young colleague of mine prescribed narcotics for his wife's migraines and caused her to become an addict. Another doctor, who could not resist his need for control, treated his children, leaving them with unnecessary, ugly scars.

I knew the risks, I was familiar with the literature: "The physician who is family lacks the gyroscope of clinical poise, an axis of objectivity in the reeling emotions of family illness."[2] And again: "The physician does not have a valid physician-patient relationship with his or her own family."[3] Knowing all this, what should I do?

My hands shook, and I perspired as I scrubbed the morning of the surgery. Once we started to work, I was able to concentrate on what we were doing and the shaking stopped. When we saw the size and extent of the tumor, there was no question of resectability. A tear ran down my cheek into my mask, but all who were working around the table were too busy to notice.

After we had closed Eva's chest, I went into the locker room to change. I surprised myself when I started to swear under my breath, very uncharacteristic for me. I was really angry and hurled my gown into the hamper rather than tossing it as I usually did. I slammed the locker door shut before I got ahold of myself and remembered that anger is one of the prominent reactions to grief and loss. I was no different, as a physician, than anyone else who found out that a family member had widely metastasized lung cancer; I was angry. I asked myself, why her? Why at her age? Why my sister?

When I visited Eva in the intensive care unit, she asked me whether we had been able to do anything. I mutely shook my head.

After getting her affairs in order, my sister moved in with my family, and I became her caretaker and physician. We had asked an internist to be her doctor and write her prescriptions, but she ignored his advice. Hypnosis, along with pain pills, controlled her distress. When she developed superior vena cava obstruction we switched to demerol and morphine. It was hard to be her sister and doctor. She would complain that the shots hurt and that I should return to medical school to learn how to do what I was

> ... I HAD WITNESSED THE TRAGIC CONSEQUENCES OF PHYSICIANS TREATING MEMBERS OF THEIR FAMILY.

doing, and the next minute we would be hugging each other and crying. Once her face started to swell, she did not want to see any other family members, including her two children, because she did not want to be remembered puffy and distorted.

My sister and patient was insistent to the end to be in charge of her surroundings and her life. She would not sleep in a hospital bed with rails, because it felt too confining—"like a jail." She had fallen out of her regular bed several times, and she was too heavy for me to pick up. We compromised and both of us slept on the floor, which she found acceptable. She decided how much, and at what time interval, she would take which medication. She smoked until the end. She decided who should visit her and when; she was in charge of arranging her flowers and ordering her menu. She became incontinent when she was near death but adamantly refused a catheter; she could not even accept that she had lost control of her bladder function. She gave her body to the medical school. She was angry at dying young, before she could make enough money to help her children finish their education.

Should I have done things differently, not assisted at her surgery, not cared for her but admitted her to a nursing home? I think not. Because of Eva's overwhelming need for control and independence, she would have been unable to fit into the compliant, passive role expected of a patient.

A stranger would have found it very difficult to extend to her the understanding and compassionate care that she sought as her life came to an end. My rule not to care for relatives, as all rules, has exceptions. Caring for Eva was an exception. ❖

References
1. La Puma J, Priest ER. Is there a doctor in the house? An analysis of the practice of physicians treating their own families. JAMA. 1992;267:1810-2.
2. Miles SH. A piece of my mind. Midnight Visiting Hour. JAMA. 1989;262:2008.
3. Boiko PE, Schuman SH, physicians treating their own spouses: relationship of physicians to their own family's health care. J Fam Pract. 1984;18:891-6.

**Renate G Justin, MD,** was in family practice with her daughter Ingrid, until both joined the Colorado Permanente Medical Group. Dr. Justin is now retired, after 45 years of practicing medicine.

**Suns**
photograph
This photograph is a multiple exposure, taken at Bathurst Inlet, on Canada's arctic coast. It shows both sunset and sunrise.

**Alexander Kleider, MD,** is a neurosurgeon with The Permanente Medical Group in Redwood City, CA.

## Scarlet Letters

*"Let her cover the mark as she will,
the pang of it will be always in her heart."*
—N Hawthorne

Your are different from us
—we who glide
through our workday unfettered
by handicaps. Genetics
have been unkind,
first one illness, then another.
The body you inhabit
at war with itself.

Your face, a map
of life events—lines carved
by medication and disease;
your torso tattooed
by steroids, gastric mucosa
stripped and acid-etched.
These side effects require
additional medication,
and a time-keeping pill box.
Remedies are few, fantasies
many: a skin which begs
to be unzipped—these are the wishes
of the helpless.

At your next office visit,
the doctor consults his oracle,
but has no further suggestions.

## Marrowstone Island

Sunset spills crimson waves
across the sand, unveiling
a crescent of tidal pools.

Our hands touch briefly—
years of understanding flow between us.
My heart beats with yours;

the tide pulses
against the ventricle of the shore;
sun's smooth pendulum measures time.

I match the rhythm
of your stride, one arm curving
around your back.

Blue herons skim across the bay
—the island already asleep,
dreaming back the tide.

Your voice,
like warm red wine,
your smile cradles a kiss.

**Sharon Carter, MD,** obtained her medical degree from Cambridge University, England. She immigrated to the US in 1979 and works for Group Health Permanente. She is a co-editor of Literary Salt, www.literarysalt.com and received a Hedgebrook residency in 2001. In 2003, she was a Jack Straw Writer. Her work may also be seen on the Internet in "Switched-on Gutenberg," and "Disquieting Muses." Visit her Web page at: www.geocities.com/Athens/Styx/6307.

## The Sleep Thief

And so what if you're tired to the bone
up all night
robbed of rest
away from home
thief phone steals large bills
of sleep you might have had
tiny bandit beeper rifles through loose change
and so what if you drag through the next morning clinic
farther and farther and farther behind
the gold ring
snatched out of your grasp
dreams for easy morning dashed
ambushed in clinic fog
and so what if you nearly fall asleep
on your way home
the highway's quiet you're finally alone
dry scratchy eyes beg to close
car wanders to and fro
driving while you nap
and so what if you nod off after dinner
feel cramped grumpy mugged
nodding snoring twisting tightly
when the alarm explodes at 5:00 the next morning
holding you up to do it again?

More information about
**J Trig Brown, MD, MPH,**
can be found on page 15.

SUMMER 1999

*soul of t*

**Châtillon-en-Bazois**

watercolor

This painting is of a chateau in Châtillon-en-Bazois, a town in the Burgundy Region of France on the Nivernais Canal.

**Douglas P Grey, MD,** is the Chief of Vascular Surgery with The Permanente Medical Group in San Francisco, CA. He is a Clinical Professor of Surgery at the University of California, San Francisco and has been painting in watercolors for over a decade.

**A Man**
acrylic

**A Woman**
acrylic

See page 35 for more
information about
**Terry Laskiewicz, MD.**

The
Permanente Journal
FALL 1999     VOLUME 3 NO. 3

*CME Category 1 Credit Now Available*

FALL 1999

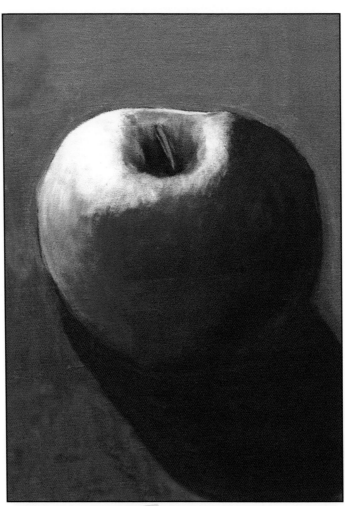

**Good Food**
acrylic

**Nooshin Farr, MD, FACP,** is a full-time
hospitalist with the Mid-Atlantic Permanente
Medical Group. She has been with Kaiser
Permanente since 1987 and served as the
Chief of Hospital Service from 1999-2004.

**My Kitchen**
acrylic

**Potomac, Maryland**
acrylic

# A Child's Last Leaf

A few years ago when the oak tree was sick
Dad insisted it had to go
she cried out with alarm, "I dance on its limbs,
talk with the squirrels and when the window's open
it whispers to me."

Dad bowed his head, "OK we'll wait."

High in the branches of the oak tree
where larks jostled offspring to wing
in September when she wasn't as well
she cradled herself in the boughs of the tree
remembering Doc's prophecy only
on chemotherapy days.

Her candle burned swiftly

for she wore fine lace and fragrance to smile.

"I won't leave you while the oak tree's got leaves,
I've counted them
It has thousands, it's still very green."

As thousands became hundreds
the leaves matched her skin,
fine porcelain stained yellow reflecting
stress cracks for relief

Then with eyes as sunken diamonds,
she beamed through her windows
carrying sorrows, and uttered,
"the last leaf hasn't fallen"

As she slept one fall night
with the wind's help
that leaf floated freely.

**Victor David, MD,** retired from The
Permanente Medical Group's Ob/Gyn
Department in Oakland, CA in 1999. He
now works as a consultant to The
Permanente Medical Group in the
Regional Call Center in Vallejo, CA.
While enjoying a new role in life, he
continues to write poetry, and has been
published in several poetry magazines.

WINTER 2000

# Brad Becker, MD

This image has no specific meaning, but I like the idea of opposites. Normally animals are in motion whereas trees and landscapes are stationary. Here I've created a sense of motion in the trees with a stationary bird.

**Clarity**
digital image
The photograph of the bird was taken in the Northern California area. The trees in the background are in a park in Dr. Becker's neighborhood.

**Ikibana**
digital image

*soul of t*

### Elimination
digital image

This image was created by cloning background elements to cover the elephant. This image is a comment on the fragility of our ecosystem.

### Ascent
digital image

This image was created as a holiday greeting card for 1998. Images of sherpas were decolorized and superimposed on a photo taken in the Everest Region of Nepal. The doorway was applied and enhanced with a photo flare to create the sense of a spiritual ascent. The hand was superimposed to capture the sense of struggle involved in life's journeys.

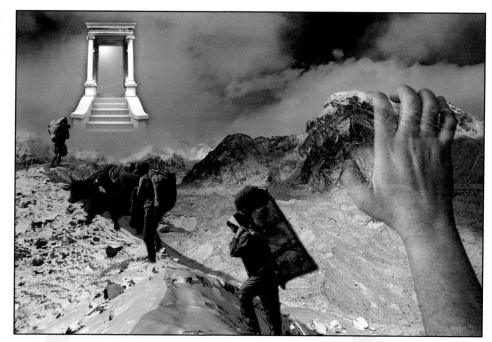

**Brad Becker, MD,** is a dermatologist with The Permanente Medical Group in Oakland, CA. He has expanded his interest in photography to digital manipulation of images.

# Michael Horberg, MD, FACP

## Out of the Closet

*Why Gay and Lesbian Doctors have an Important Role to Play in Healthcare*

Finding the place to begin talking about being a doctor and being gay is not an easy thing for me. I am both. And it is this "same-sex marriage" that defines both who I am and the kind of doctor I've become.

I knew I wanted to be a doctor since I was five years old. For one thing, the patriarch of my family (my uncle) was a physician. And then too there was my grandmother, who, just before she died, gave me my first medical kit as a birthday present. As I recall, I slipped the toy stethoscope that was included in the kit around my neck and asked a relative to cough.

It was the cough that launched a career.

Thirteen years later, Boston University accepted me into their six-year medical program. Then I returned to the town I had grown up in, Chicago, to do an internal medicine residency at Michael Reese Hospital. It was an ordeal all right—the long hours, the challenging patients, the academic rigors of residency. But compared to coming to terms with my homosexuality, the whole process of going through medical school and internship was a piece of cake.

It was about two years after that momentous fifth birthday that I just spoke about that in some vague, undeniable way, I got my first inkling that I was different. Of course, I didn't have a word for it, and even when I did, I didn't do anything about it until near the end of medical school. And I stayed in "the closet" a few more years after that. The AIDS epidemic (or gay-related immunodeficiency as it was known back then) I'm sure had something to do with this prolonged reticence. For it gave those who were already homophobic a powerful new focus. And while certainly AIDS patients did receive compassionate care from the medical mainstream during those years, an undercurrent of prejudice did nevertheless surface—especially among my older colleagues. So, at least from a professional standpoint, staying in the closet seemed like a smart idea.

However, around the time that I entered private practice, there were a couple of things that happened that changed my attitude. First, my gay and lesbian friends began using me as their doctor, and, by word-of-mouth, I soon drew others. My willingness to be out, and their ability to come out, meant that they were finally getting the care and attention that they so desperately yearned for but didn't think they had gotten. And I, in turn, became increasingly attuned to their unique health needs and concerns. (I should add that as my practice within the community became better known, I drew more straight patients as well.)

Secondly, and more sadly, as the AIDS epidemic worsened, a growing number of the patients I treated were being diagnosed with HIV. As traditional therapies failed, I aggressively sought alternatives. I enrolled them in stage three trials for ddI, ddC, d4t, and all the other drugs that would follow. And the more active I became, the more calls I received from pharmaceutical reps who, obviously enough, were just as eager as I was to see their latest AIDS drugs tested out.

And so I was drawn farther and farther out of the closet. So far out, in fact, that by 1994, I became a member of the board of the Gay and Lesbian Medical Association (GLMA) and in that capacity began to shamelessly "out" myself to anyone I thought might be a potential GLMA member. Also that same year, I became president of Gay and Lesbian Physicians of Chicago.

Coming out was an extremely liberating experience for me. There was no hiding anymore; I was true to the world, and it was true to me. And it paid off in any number of ways. For one thing, because I was a gay doctor with a large gay and lesbian patient population, Northwestern Community Medical Group (affiliated with Northwestern Memorial Hospital) invited me to merge my practice with theirs. And because I had a high patient satisfaction rating, managed care companies came courting as well.

I moved to the Bay Area in 1997 and now practice internal and HIV Medicine for Kaiser Permanente in Santa Clara. Here, I've been completely accepted and respected by my colleagues. And that has been very gratifying, indeed.

However, if there's one moral to be gleaned from my story, it's this: medicine is not a popularity contest, it is a dialogue in mutual respect and dignity. And, in this regard, gay and lesbian doctors have much to offer.

Medicine and gay rights are both my life's work. And if we ever meet, don't be afraid to ask me about either. I'm out about both 24 hours a day, seven days a week. Too bad I'm not paid an hourly wage. ❖

*Reprinted by permission of the publisher from California Medicine, 1997 Nov; 8(9):44.*

**Michael Horberg, MD, FACP,** practices HIV and internal medicine for The Permanente Medical Group in Santa Clara, CA. He co-chairs the KPNCR HIV Provider and Therapeutics Subcommittee and is a past president of the national Gay and Lesbian Medical Association.

The Permanente Journal

SPRING 2000    VOLUME 4 NO. 2

SPRING 2000

*be healer*

YOSEMITE IS
A FAVORITE
PLACE TO
SPEND TIME.

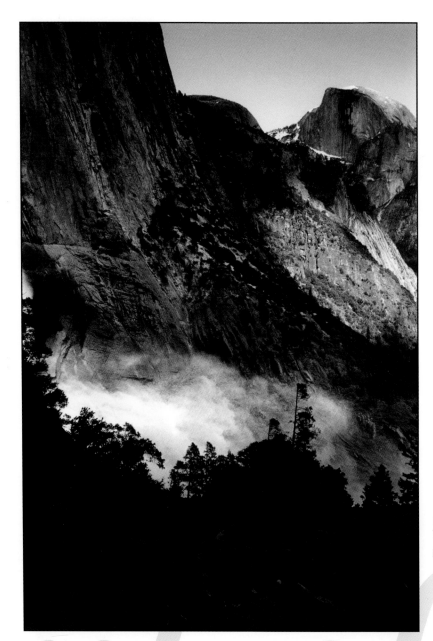

**Half Dome from the
Yosemite Falls Trail**

photograph

*soul of t*

**Peacock at the Window**
photograph

**Cats' Hill Criterium**
photograph

**J Richard Gaskill, MD,** is an otolaryngologist with The Permanente Medical Group in Santa Clara, CA. His interests include biking, hiking, climbing, photography, travel, and writing poetry.

SUMMER 2000

*soul of t*

I CREDIT
MY MEDICAL
KNOWLEDGE FOR
ENHANCING
MY ART.

**A Friday Walk**
acrylic
Recalls Dr. Osman's life
in Somalia: a family
heads to the golden
white beach of the
Indian Ocean, a luxury
of living near a coast.

**Mohamed Osman, MD,** was a physician with Group Health Permanente.
He is now a full-time artist living in North Carolina. He was born in Somalia;
his life there is a major influence in his art. Dr. Osman is a self-taught artist.
His work has appeared in group and solo exhibitions. His Web site is rated
by Google as number one in the world for the category of contemporary
African art. Visit his Web site at: www.osmanart.homestead.com.

KATE SCANNELL, MD

# Women in Medicine—A Living History

*The remarkable career of Dr. Ellen Killebrew shines a light on the history of women in medicine, as illuminated by this testimonial to her on the occasion of her retirement from TPMG in 1999.*

We gather tonight to honor Dr. Ellen Killebrew during this major transition in her life—one that also marks a transition for every person in this room. The impressive number of women doctors assembled here attests to the fact of Ellen's considerable impact on each of us. How often does any occasion draw so many of us from our busy professional and personal lives?

As we approach the new millennium, it is fitting that we pay tribute to Ellen—both for her stellar individual accomplishments and for her obstinate insistence on being a physician. Her career embodies the broader historical context of women in medicine, and each time that she challenged the barriers excluding women from medicine, she made things easier for the next group of women who had to confront them. Her impact on us has been both personal and professional.

The "official and usual" facts of Ellen's career are these: That tonight we celebrate an outstanding clinician and teacher, a gifted cardiologist, a Clinical Professor of Medicine at the University of California at San Francisco, a long-standing officer of the American Heart Association, a published author of medical works, and a respected colleague who has worked 28 years for Kaiser Permanente (KP).

However, as always, the facts are never simple, and they are inherently thin. What expands the facts of Ellen's career into an experience that has affected each of us is the particular way in which she negotiated her career through the difficult history of women in American medicine. Most of Ellen's career was lived through periods of time when professional barriers to women were pervasive and blatantly prejudicial. Remarkably, Ellen not only endured those times—through her persistence and her perennial mentoring and support of other women physicians who followed her—but she also helped to reshape the landscape for other women who would later enter medicine.

Looking around the room, we see an intergenerational group of women doctors whose careers span the last half-century of American medical history—some have recently completed their medical residencies. By comparison, it is interesting to note that in 1968, when Ellen finished her residency at Colorado General Hospital, no other women were seated at the commencement table. Things were

a little better in 1983 when I completed mine in Chicago; yet while there were six other women in my residency program, we were—"treated" to a female striptease dancer as the main entertainment for our commencement ceremony.

In 1955, Ellen entered Bucknell University in Pennsylvania to pursue a business major and become an executive secretary, one of the few acceptable academic majors available to women then. However, during her sophomore year, she decided to enter premedical training. Her decision constituted a radical act at the time. In fact, the university mandated that Ellen obtain written permission from her father as a strict prerequisite for enrolling in premedical courses. How many of us here tonight can imagine being told that our fathers had the right to determine what we could study and what we could become?

It is instructive to read about this time in history in Hedda Garza's book, *Women in Medicine*. She writes: "By 1955, a new low point had been reached. Many medical schools that had welcomed women during the war no longer had a single female student. Now that women were no longer needed, polls were published to justify the sudden change. In 1949 and 1957, hospital chiefs of staff and male physicians gave familiar answers to the questionnaires asking them their opinions of female doctors. Many of them commented that women doctors were 'emotionally unstable,' 'talk too much' and 'get pregnant.' One dean actually declared that he preferred a third-rate man to a first rate woman doctor."[1]

When I asked Ellen about her experiences in premedical training, she said that she often had to endure dreary, misogynist attitudes. Among the most painful memories, she recalled being charged with cheating on her biochemistry exam simply because a woman was not expected to excel as she had. Male students raided her dorm room looking for evidence to support their accusations, which were, of course, false.

In 1960, just one year after Ellen completed her premedical training, Jefferson Medical College in Pennsylvania finally opened its doors to women and became the last medical school in the United States forced to do so. Still, during her medical school interviews, Ellen was asked why she wanted to "take a man's place." She was also queried as to whether she had thought about having a family and, consequently, about expecting to drop out of medical school.

The prejudicial atmosphere that prevailed while Ellen attended the New Jersey College of Medicine was reflected in the 1962 writings of historian Frederick Rudolph. He congratulated the male colleges like Yale and Harvard for "preserving the liberal inheritance of Western Civilization in the United States by protecting it from debilitating, feminizing, corrupting influences which shaped its career where coeducation prevailed."[1]

Despite this formidable climate, Ellen graduated from medical school in 1965 when, still, only 4.6% of all women with an MD degree had become full-time medical school faculty members.[2] When she completed her internal medicine residency at Colorado General and Denver General Hospital three years later, three fourths of the three million health care workers in this country were women, while nearly all administrators and physicians were men. Only 7% of physicians were women—a negligible difference from the 6% figure in 1900.[1] In 1970—only after The Women's Equity Action League filed a class action suit on behalf of all women against every medical college in the country—the United States Congress finally held its first hearings on the incontestable gender inequality in medical school admissions. And in 1970, while these difficulties prevailed, Ellen Killebrew finished her cardiology Fellowship at the Pacific Medical Center in San Francisco.

In that same year, Ellen's first venture into the job market brought her to the doors of KP San Francisco where she was told that they were not hiring "women cardiologists." The physicians operating two private practices told her the same thing. But Ellen persevered and ultimately broke through several additional barriers at Richmond and Oakland KP to obtain employment. In her true pioneering fashion, her successful fight to secure employment just preceded passage of the Equal Opportunity Act in 1971, a legislation that forced open the doors of professional education for all women in this country.

While Ellen was on her way to becoming one of the most respected physicians at Oakland KP, formidable odds continued to mark the general medical landscape for women. In a study published in 1974, two-thirds of practicing male physicians did not accept women as peers.[3] That same year, another study revealed that 80% of New York City medical patients stated their preference for a male physician, although half had never been treated by a woman.[4] In 1982, JAMA published an article entitled, "Attitudes towards Women Physicians in Medical Academia" which reported that almost 50% of male medical students and physicians agreed with this statement: "Women physicians who spend long hours at work are neglecting their responsibilities to home and family."[5] In a survey published one year later in the American Journal of Psychiatry, 30% of male physicians felt, "There was a significant risk to the optimal functioning of a department that hired a woman of child-bearing age."[6]

Many women in this room remember arriving at KP Oakland in the late 1980s and sensing immediate reassurance from Ellen's welcoming presence. Senior women physicians were scarce in the 80s. By 1981, but for a single post that had been held at the Women's Medical College of Pennsylvania in 1955, no woman had yet to hold a chief administrative position (such as full dean).[1] As late as 1985, women accounted for only 5% of medical school professors,[7] and in 1988, only 15% of active MDs.[1]

Perhaps as remarkable as her private and professional struggles is the style in which Ellen practiced medicine and expanded her career. She bore no malice for the hardships that she endured, and she never begrudged the success of other women who did not have to suffer them.

On the contrary, Ellen always took time to mentor any woman who approached her with professional or personal issues. She was a rare exception to Janet Bickel's 1988 proclamation in "Women in Medical Education": "There are few departments in any school in which a student can readily find a woman physician in a senior position who is happy with both her professional life and her personal life and available to give the student pointers and support."[8]

We enter the new Millennium with some new "facts." In the 1998-9 academic year, women comprised 44% of medical school entrants and 15% of cardiology fellows,[9] and, by 2010, it is predicted that women will

THOSE WHO NOW SAY THAT BEING A WOMAN IN MEDICINE "IS NO BIG DEAL" CAN DO SO ONLY FROM THE POSITION OF PRIVILEGE MADE POSSIBLE BY THE EFFORTS OF WOMEN LIKE ELLEN KILLEBREW.

account for 30% of practicing physicians.[10] Still, in 1995, a national cohort study showed that after 11 years, only 5% of women had achieved full professorship status, compared with 23% of men with similar initial rank, type of tenure track, and board certification.[11] Additionally, women comprise only 7% of all full professorships in internal medicine.[12]

While the numbers of women in medicine and leadership positions continue to lag behind those for men, other forms of gender discrimination also continue. In her book, *Walking out on the Boys*, Francis K Conley, MD, of Stanford University wrote about some modern day varieties of sexual inequality in medicine: "I have learned that universities, in general, no longer function as agents of societal change.... [that their] liberal environment is a masquerade."[13] In 1994, a report in the *New England Journal of Medicine* documented a harassment rate of 73% among women responding to a survey about sexual harassment in medical training.[14]

Within the sociopolitical context of women in medicine, Ellen has been a genuine hero. She braved formidable barriers in her path to becoming a physician and, in so doing, helped to pave an easier entry for other women who followed. When we look to Ellen and recognize her brilliance and her rightful place in medicine, it is painful to think about the abuse and the misogyny she was made to endure.

Those who now say that being a woman in medicine "is no big deal" can do so only from the position of privilege made possible by the efforts of women like Ellen Killebrew. The fact is that being a woman in medicine *has always been* a big deal to the rest of society.

Each of us has arrived here in a long procession of women which widens in rank by the years. And near the leading edge of the procession is Ellen Killebrew—pioneering and pulling many of us along. We honor her tonight for her courageous and generous leadership, her inspired mentoring, her indisputable clinical skills, her unselfconscious wisdom, and her personal and professional integrity. We thank her for being one of the rare women in a senior position who was happy with her career and life and who offered her own happiness as a beacon for many of us who were looking for some light in our careers. We thank her for helping us to create and integrate a professional identity.

And finally, on a personal note that I know to be shared by many others here, I also want her to know how much her vivacity and wit delighted me. And, simply, how much I will miss her. ❖

References
1. Garza H. Women in medicine. New York: Franklin Watts, Publisher; 1994.
2. Eisenberg C. Medicine is no longer a man's profession. N Engl J Med 1989;321:1542-4.
3. Standley S, Soule B. Women in professions: Historic antecedents and current lifestyles. In: Hardy RE, Cull JC (eds): Career Guidance for Young Women. Springfield, IL: Charles C Thomas, Publisher; 1974.
4. Marieskind HI. Women in the Health System. St Louis: CV Mosby Co; 1980.
5. Scadron A, Witte MH, Axelrod M, Greenberg EA, Arem C, Mertz JE. Attitudes towards women in medical academia. JAMA 1982;247:2803-7.
6. Franco K, Evans CL, Best AP, Zrull JP, Pizza GA. Conflicts associated with physicians' pregnancies. Amer J Psychiatry 1983;140:902-4.
7. Graves PL, Thomas CB. Correlates of midlife career achievement among women physicians. JAMA 1985;254:781-7.
8. Bickel J. Women in medical education. N Engl J Med1988;319:1579-84.
9. Barzansky B, Jonas HS, Etzel SI. Graduate medical education. JAMA 1999;282:840-6.
10. Frank E, McMurray JE, Linzer M, Elon L. Career satisfaction of US women physicians. Results from the Women Physicians' Health Study. Arch Intern Med 1999;159:1417-26.
11. Tesch BJ, Wood HM, Helwig AL, Nattinger AB. Promotion of women physicians in academic medicine: glass ceiling or sticky floor? JAMA 1995;273:1022-5.
12. Association of American Medical Colleges. Increasing women's leadership in academic medicine. Washington, DC: Association of American Colleges; 1996.
13. Conley FK. Walking out on the boys. New York: Farrar, Straus, and Giroux; 1998.
14. Komaromy M, Bindman AB, Haber RJ, Sande M. Sexual harassment in medical training. N Engl J Med 1993;328:322-6.

**Kate Scannell, MD,** is an internist, rheumatologist, and geriatrician with The Permanente Medical Group in Oakland, CA. She is author of the book, "Death of the Good Doctor" and a columnist for the Oakland Tribune/ANG Newspapers. She also edits *Ethics Rounds* for Kaiser Permanente.

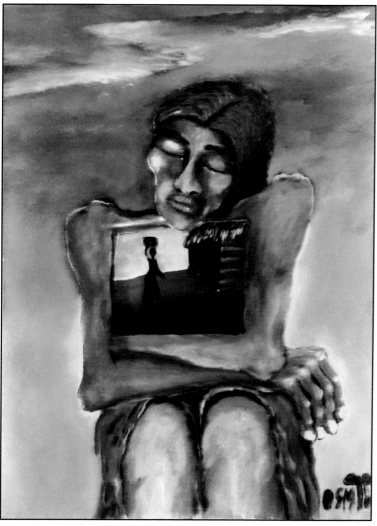

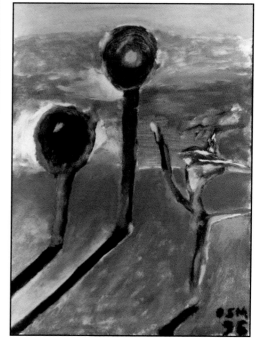

**Life on Mars**

acrylic

Imaginary figures on Mars, a
planet prone to excitement and
mystery yet to be discovered.

**Dream**

acrylic

An expression of a content, quasi-happy face in a
sleeping woman voyaging through space and time.

More information about
**Mohamed Osman, MD,**
can be found on page 59.

**Parental Respect**
acrylic
A daughter's reluctance to keep straight eye contact with her mother signifies a formal gesture of respect in many cultures.

More information about **Mohamed Osman, MD,** can be found on page 59.

*soul of t*

64

# In the Shadow of Obesity (Part I)

## Introduction

I remember that in the first decade of my career, if I had a 300-pound patient on my exam table, I would desperately have been searching my mind to find something other than the obvious to discuss. The possibility of considering why a person was obese was inconceivable; it was totally out of the question. The edge of an abyss was not something I was about to approach in a naive and inquiring manner. Why would I risk leaving the security of conventional medical knowledge to learn by observation and inquiry of what was before me?

And yet, years later I was to wonder why do people get fat? Where in nature is obesity? Why are so many obese adults born prematurely at low weights? What does it mean that a recently seen 850-pound, 29-year-old woman was one of the first long-term survivors of severe prematurity just under two pounds at birth? Should we even think about this? Is this medicine? It certainly has nothing to do with what we learned in medical school and residency. Isn't it better to read about intermediary neurotransmitters and obesity, especially if one doesn't think about the implication of "intermediary" or "transmitter"?

On the following pages are four photographs taken by Eric Blau, MD, an internist with Southern California Permanente Medical Group and an accomplished professional photographer. His efforts in medical photojournalism have already been reviewed in a recent book column of *The Permanente Journal*. These photographs, intermediary transmitters in their own way, will someday appear as part of a book he is now working on that provides the patients' views of their obesity, but only to those physicians who dare ask.

– Vincent J Felitti, MD

## A note from physician and photographer, Eric Blau, MD

As a society, we spend millions of dollars annually in a mostly futile attempt to lose weight. In a culture already obsessed by health and youth, we tend to discriminate against the overweight among us, finding them lazy, out of control, and lacking willpower. As physicians, we reinforce these cultural models by pointing out to our overweight patients the health risks of obesity. Clearly, the ideal of beauty is not that of the overweight: fashionable clothing is created for the thin.

It is always a revelation when information becomes available to make me rethink basic paradigms of medicine. My training and most of the current literature on obesity led me to believe that morbidly obese people had abnormalities that probably were genetically acquired. I thought it was only a matter of time before these would be characterized and medications developed to alleviate the suffering of millions of Americans.

When I first learned of the Adverse Childhood Experiences (ACE) study and the relation between abuse and morbid obesity, I was shocked and skeptical that it was true. But after interviewing dozens of morbidly obese individuals, I am a believer. Over and over again, I would hear people state that they overeat well past the point of satisfaction usually in response to some psychological trauma. It appears all too frequently that marked weight gain began with trauma, and becomes a habituated reaction to new life stresses. Obesity is a complex disorder and not all overweight persons have been traumatized, but unless one is aware that at least a large percentage of the grossly overweight have had severe emotional trauma, it is unlikely that successful therapies will be devised.

Rather than argue the case myself, I would prefer to let some overweight persons tell their own stories. These are excerpts from interviews that focused on how being overweight has affected their lives, and how their lives have affected being overweight.

"With my friend, Paul, the manner of this passing was not a sudden thing. Paul and I were in Air Force Pararescue in Vietnam. We grew up together in Oakland, went to the same schools, enlisted together, and ended in Pararescue together. Our job was to rescue downed pilots, patch them together, and get them medevaced to a facility that could do something for them. We had a rotating schedule of rescues. On that particular day, I was at the top of the list for missions, but I had an impacted wisdom tooth, so I spent the day with the base dentist having it removed. My best friend, Paul, ended up going on a mission that I should have drawn. He never came back from it.

It took almost two weeks for us to find him. I went in after him several times: I volunteered for every outbound mission in his direction. We found him spread-eagled between two trees and skinned alive. There was only one thing that was recognizable about him, and they made sure that it was—that was his face. They left that intact. They didn't touch it a bit. The rest of him looked like something you'd find in a slaughterhouse.

I got weird for a while. I spent a lot of time dwelling on the fact that my friend died over there. I became a risk-taker. I increased my smoking to eight packs of cigarettes per day and it hasn't changed, it's just gone in a different direction. I have morbid obesity, advanced cardiovascular disease, diabetes, and limited respiratory function. Do you see a pattern here?

Everybody looks at the downside of obesity, of alcoholism, or drug abuse. But there is an upside, too. There has to be, or people wouldn't do it."

— "JP" 400+ pounds

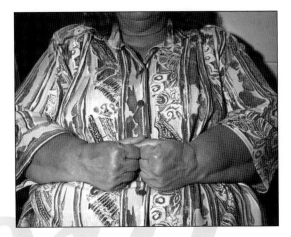

"When I was young, about four I think, I was molested by a teenage boy. After that, my mother would often call me in the house from playing, pull down my clothes, and check me out; it was humiliating. Later, when I was growing up, I was labeled mentally retarded, and men used to think they could do things to me and no one would believe me.

When I am stressed, I eat. Food is my friend; it's there for me. Especially because my family isn't. I don't eat because I'm hungry I'm never hungry. I eat because it's there. If it's cake, I'll eat it 'til it's gone even if I'm feeling full. I feel good when I'm eating it. But after awhile, I realize that I can't eat enough to stop the pain."

— Ella Herman, 300+ pounds

"I was rather slender until I was seven years old. Beginning about that time I was sexually abused by my father. It continued until I was fourteen. I never told anybody. He kept telling me it was our secret and that I shouldn't tell anybody. In junior high school I realized how taboo this was and how I could actually get pregnant. I was terrified! It was then that I put a stop to it. I had a very low opinion of myself. I think children who are abused somehow think it is their fault. I felt guilty and that I was not terribly worthwhile. I weighed two hundred pounds then.

I've recognized that I always eat when I'm lonesome, unhappy, or hurt. And I spent a lot of time hurt by other people who didn't realize that I was hurt. I'd seem like this jolly person, and then I'd go home and cry half the night and eat. I'm a binge eater. I can sit down with a box of cookies and eat the whole box I think because I'm alone. And I eat even when I'm full. I've eaten a package of cookies even when it's made me sick to my stomach. But I'd continue to eat them because they tasted good I guess."

— Helen McClure, 258 pounds

"No matter what you do to your face, your body is still there. I'm a hairdresser. I can make my hair look fabulous. I do great makeup. I look good without makeup: I'm an attractive female. I'm intelligent, I'm energetic, but it doesn't matter because below the neck I am who I am. And that's hard because even though you as an individual may not be superficial, society truly is. And I don't know if it's just that our society has become more superficial in other ways, too. Maybe we're a culture of teenagers.

Food doesn't give you a hard time. Food doesn't create arguments. It doesn't talk. My favorite food when I'm unhappy is pasta with my Mom's homemade sauce."

— Karen McWhorter, 220 pounds

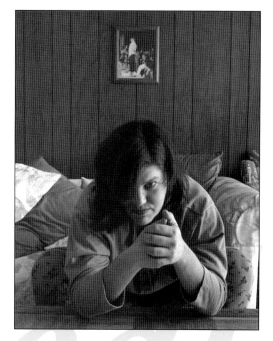

For more information about **Eric Blau, MD,** see page 27.

Permanente Journal

FALL 2000    VOLUME 4 NO. 4

*Complete our Reader Survey
and enter a drawing to win
one of three great prizes.*

KAISER PERMANENTE

FALL 2000

*soul of t*

**Boats on Lake Titicaca**
photograph

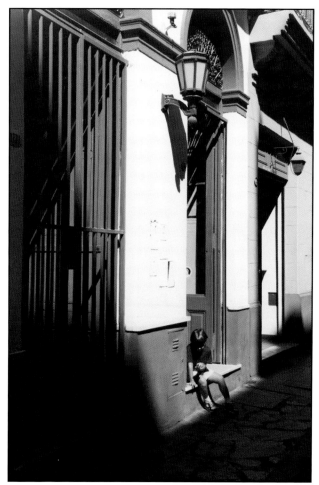

**Doorstep Child**
photograph
This picture was taken on
a side street in the San
Telmo section of Buenos
Aires, Argentina.

**Udo Wahn, MD,** is an Ob/Gyn with the
Southern California Permanente Medical
Group in San Diego, CA. He is the author
of *A Woman's Guide to Surgical Options in
the New Millennium: A Gentler Approach,*
and he co-author of *Your Guys Guide to
Gynecology.* Dr. Wahn enjoys surfing,
camping, mountain biking, and being a dad.

RENATE G JUSTIN, MD

# House Calls

Patients enter my space when they come to my office; I enter their space when I go to their homes. I am invited into my patients' kitchens, living rooms, and lives when I make house calls. Patients learn about me by observing the ambience of my waiting room; I learn about them by observing the colors, furnishings, art, and books in their dwellings. Once in their home, I may perceive, within minutes, what eludes me in the examination room. When I pick my way carefully to an elderly man's bedroom, along a narrow path bordered on both sides with walls of piled-up newspapers, I at once understand the severity of his neurosis, which escapes me when I concentrate on his coronary artery disease in the office. A glance into the refrigerator, while getting a cold drink of water, tells me more about my patient's diet than I will find out by exhaustive questioning.

When we stop making house calls, we lose the intimacy of the relationship in which doctors and patients alternate being hosts. Displaying family pictures on the desk is not exclusively the doctor's privilege; patients also can share photographs when the physician visits in their home. The balance of power in the doctor-patient relationship shifts by changing the locale of the encounter from office to home.

House calls can be surprising, frightening, sad, and, at times, inspiring. House calls make me feel humble because they teach me under what adverse conditions the human spirit can survive and even thrive. I also learn things about my patients of which I stay ignorant if I only see them in the office. A grand piano in the home of a lady who has hypertension and is no longer allowed to drive because of epilepsy leads me to ask her if she would play for me. I am deeply moved by the beauty of the music and her expertise. Both of us momentarily forget the reason for my visit and revel in the joyous sound.

House calls can also arouse pity. A childless couple, Mr. and Mrs. Peters, have been patients for several years. Both hold jobs in spite of Mr. Peters' excess use of alcohol. One sunny day, a neighbor of the Peters' calls to say that she is concerned about them. Their car is in the driveway, and she has not seen either Mr. or Mrs. Peters leave for work. During my lunch hour, I check on my patients. Their house looks disheveled, beer cans scattered among the weeds in the yard, the door ajar. The unkempt appearance of the yard, however, does not prepare me for the scene that confronts me as I enter. Two human forms, on iron bedsprings, covered completely with worn sheets, rats scuttling across the floor, beer bottles and empty cans piled high, enmeshed in spider webs. I gently pull back the sheet from the head of one of the prone figures, expecting a corpse. Under the sheet lies Mrs. Peters; the other sheet covers Mr. Peters. Both are breathing air that reeks of alcohol, both passed out. Carefully I re-place the sheets, as pity and pessimism overcome me. I realize that my ability to help this couple is minimal, the scope of their problems overwhelming. I am surprised, because, prior to this visit, I did not know that Mrs. Peters, as well as her husband, has severe difficulties with alcohol; knowing this makes it clear to me why controlling Mrs. Peters' blood sugar has been unusually difficult. When I bill Mr. Peters for the house call, he objects. He is unaware that I had been to his house; only my accurate description of the scenery convinces him that my bill is justified. During this discussion, my offer to support him and his wife in any and all efforts to overcome their addiction is firmly and politely rejected.

The element of surprise is ubiquitous in house calls. Sixty-eight-year-old Mrs. Gerad has been in chronic mild heart failure for months. She leaves a message with the office nurse that her shortness of breath is getting worse and is told to expect me after office hours. When I arrive, Mrs. Gerad is lying in bed, obviously dyspneic, with distended neck veins. I suggest she sit up to ease her breathing and therefore put a sofa pillow under her back. While fluffing up her bed pillow I feel something hard, a loaded revolver. I am scared and taken aback, but on further reflection, I realize that this weapon is meant to protect my helpless patient against unwelcome intruders. It might well have discharged while I rearranged the pillows, but I leave it where I found it, and resolve to be more careful in the future.

Usually I do not make house calls to a stranger. However, a concerned neighbor is desperate and insistent; therefore, I tell her I will come. From the appearance of the small, ramshackle house, I conclude that the owner has been sick for some time. The portly, white-haired lady who called me greets me on her doorstep. She reports that her neighbor has been moaning loudly all night and adamantly refuses to go to the emergency room.

My knocks go unanswered. When I open the door slowly so as not to startle anyone, a strong smell of vomit assails me. I leave the door open to let in some fresh air; it is too early in the year to worry about flies following me in. The curtains are drawn, but a weak bulb sheds enough light to reveal a man, about sixty-four, in bed with a shotgun leaning against the bedframe. He greets me loudly: "Who the h… are you?" From the tenor of his voice, I conclude that he is deaf and therefore respond equally loudly that I am a doctor who has come at his neighbor's request. "D… meddler," he comments. After my eyes adjust to the dim light, I see the outline of the man's greatly distended abdomen under the sheet. He is undoubtedly obstructed, given the pain, distention, and vomiting. "Do you want me to examine your stomach?" I query. He pulls down the sheet. He is fully dressed but has unzipped his pants to allow for the distention. I do not have a chance to lay a hand on him because he starts to retch and moan. When, exhausted, he lies back, he looks at me as if he has forgotten our previous exchange. In a hoarse but loud voice, he says: "What do you think you are doing here? Get the h… out." At which point, he starts to reach for his gun. I hasten to tell him again who I am and that I have come to help ease his pain. "None of your d… business!" In my bag are a few demerol and codeine tablets, which I leave on his nightstand next to a glass of murky water. "You may take these if the pain gets too bad; your neighbor has my telephone number if you want me to return." He responds: "I told you to get the h… out of here." I do just that.

I never heard from the neighbor nor from the old man with the gun again. That he could not accept the help I offered, but insisted on suffering alone in his smelly, semi-dark room made me sad, but also I was frightened by his gun, his anger. Driving away from that scene, I wondered about this man's life, his job, his family. What experiences made it impossible for him to accept help, or even to acknowledge that help was being offered in good faith? Also I mulled over my own actions. Would a different approach have been more successful? If I had moved the gun out of his reach when I entered, I would have been less threatened by him; and perhaps if I had stayed longer, he would have relaxed more in my presence? Should I go back and try again, or was it now too dangerous?

Years ago, a young woman called me to the home of her grandmother, who was in pain. The old lady lived in a one-room, wooden cabin. When I entered, she was stretched out on a narrow bed, softly moaning, but she greeted me in a warm, welcoming manner. The source of her pain was a large, creeping cancer, that had eaten away part of her face. She was small, frail, and her thin body left enough room for me to sit down on the edge of her mattress and hold her hand while I explained how to use the medicines I left for her. Her granddaughter took notes, and when I was finished, we three women held hands silently for a few minutes in that small cabin. I left after a gentle hug with both the young and the old woman, and with a renewed respect for, and joy in the human spirit. The dignity and quietude with which death was expected by this woman was inspiring; she had lived her life and left no major tasks unfinished.

It was different for Helen, the young mother who was dying of breast cancer. She struggled to stay alive; she wanted to celebrate her son's third birthday. She cried, inconsolable, in my arms, unable to accept her fate. Before she died, she asked me to see her son, Thomas, regularly, whether or not he was sick. I promised.

About four years after Helen's death, I once again visited Thomas, now six years old. He knew me well and, on this occasion, introduced me to his "new mom." He showed me the house into which he had recently moved with his dad and his stepmother. Once in his room, he sat down on a beanbag and told me to sit in the rocking chair. Soon he inched closer and closer to the rocking chair, and then, taking a photograph of his mother off the shelf, he sat in my lap. "Tell me about Mom."

I had known her for longer than he had and could talk to him about how pretty she was as a teenager, and how smart. "She used to come to my office even before she knew your dad. After college, your mom got a good job and then met your dad. She was a happy, lovely bride, and Thomas, your grandparents loved your dad."

I told Thomas about the breast cancer and how sick his mother had been during the chemotherapy treatment, but that she and dad really wanted him to become part of their family. He was born when his mom felt better. "Your mom and dad had two wonderful, happy years with you until mom got sick again and died."

Thomas was now snuggled in my arms, and we rocked silently for a while; then he jumped down and went out to play. I sat there alone, thinking about his lovely young mother who did not want to die. Then I left the house, content that Thomas' dad had found a new partner and a "new mom" for his son. This family no longer needed to be followed by me. Thomas and his father had recovered after Helen's death. The new family was well established; the old, deep wounds had healed. After this visit, I stopped mourning for Helen. The task she had given me, to check on Thomas, was completed. I could let go, say my final goodbye. Home visits can be healing for physicians as well as for patients.

House calls are not part of today's urban medical practice; not cost- or time-effective, they have all but disappeared from the daily routine of physicians. There are occasional articles urging the revival of house calls,[1] and even a movement to create yet another specialty, home-care doctors,[2] but it is likely that physicians will be dispensing medical care in hospitals, emergency rooms, and offices rather than in the home during the next few years. Having practiced during a time when house calls were part of every day's schedule, as well as more recently, when I did not make any house calls, I feel strongly that I dispensed better patient care when house calls were part of my work. ❖

References
1. Giovino JM. House calls: taking the practice to the patient. Fam Pract Manage 2000 Jun;7(6):49-54.
2. Guariglia V. House calls seen poised to make a comeback. Physicians Financial News 2000 Jul 7;42-3.

See page 40 for more information about **Renate G Justin, MD.**

I WAS BORN IN SOMALIA;
MY LIFE THERE IS A MAJOR
INFLUENCE IN MY ART.

**Mood Disorder**
acrylic

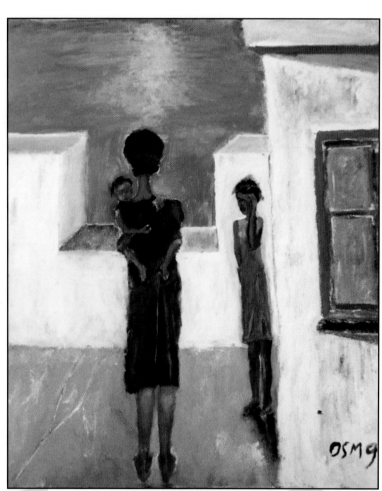

**Hope**
acrylic

More information about
**Mohamed Osman, MD,**
can be found on page 59.

*soul of t.*

# In the Shadow of Obesity (Part 2)

*Dr. Blau's striking photographs of obese patients and the quotes from his patient interviews struck a responsive chord in many readers (see page 65). To continue with the use of art in medicine, here is a diptych from a patient I asked to draw me a picture of what was inside a fat person. Following that are some clinic notes from the medical record of a man who had become obese. The autobiographical writing he supplied me as part of his treatment plan speaks for itself.*

*—Vincent J Felitti, MD*

"I was born to a 16-year-old mother whose troubled marriage soon dissolved. My father remarried shortly to a woman who did not want me; he then died when I was five. My mother became alcoholic. When I was five, I was molested by a teenaged boy babysitter. At the age of ten, I was seduced into intercourse by a 19-year-old boy, who was a babysitter's son.

I started putting on weight in ninth grade. I went to college and became a teacher. I remain celibate and smoke heavily. I have struggled with depression for years . . ."

Draw me a picture …

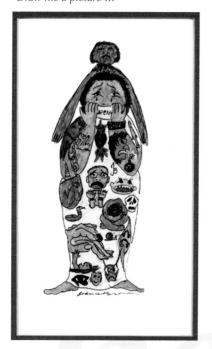

## Found in the Medical Record
## of an Obese Man — Edwin X 1/15/99

In brief, patient grew up in a large family that his mother's relatives rendered unhappy by the ramifications of "… everyone understood that my mother had married significantly below herself." He repeatedly mentions that he grew up fearing that expectations would be raised that he could not meet. He went to college and became a naval pilot. He did well and married happily but was nevertheless a 2 ppd smoker. His weight maintained at about 200 pounds until he stopped smoking and gained some.

The major event in his life was his wife's breast cancer, cerebral metastases, and her death in home hospice that he carried out for five months and by which he was overwhelmed. Asked of what she died, he tells me that although the death certificate states cerebral metastases, it was "… I believe really from leukoencephalopathy from the radiation." He gained to 300 pounds after her death and became markedly withdrawn and depressed. Sleep disturbance with myoclonic jerks and "restless legs" coincided. Ultimately, he was treated with Klonopin and 40 mg of Prozac, which have helped significantly but partially.

He tells me that on Dec 20 he created "… a big event by giving a party: it was my stepping out after being a recluse; the first time since my wife died (in 1995)." He has been unable to sleep ever since. "I feel if I just had a full stomach I'd be able to sleep, and so I get up and eat."

Patient has strong ties to the Episcopal Church; he is interested in Jungian psychology; and is a thoughtfull man. He speaks meaningfully of "inner voices." He thwarted my discussion of options in the further treatment of depression, so I asked him to provide me autobiographical writing of his wife's illness and death, to read Jaynes' *The Origin of Consciousness*, and to return in three weeks. Ultimately, he might be a good candidate for hypnotherapy. Meanwhile, he will accomplish little in the weight program until the underlying problems are resolved.

## On Jean's Death (autobiographical writing by Edwin X)

One thing to remember is that Jean was meticulous about her health. Her mother died of cancer, and Jean and I took care of her (with Hospice help) during her final months, and she had a great deal of pain. Jean kept her weight down, monitored her cholesterol, had mammograms as recommended by Kaiser, had her shots kept up to date, her teeth kept in excellent condition, etc, etc, etc. She had a hysterectomy as recommended when numerous fibrous growths were found in her uterus. And she performed routine, thorough self-examinations, during one of which she found a very small lump in her left breast.

She went to the doctor promptly, and a biopsy showed the lump to be malignant—but very small. After careful discussion, reading, and much thought, she opted for a modified radical mastectomy, which was performed promptly. No signs were found of the cancer spreading, and all the lymph nodes were clear. She was put on hormonal therapy and given periodic blood tests.

Something over a year later on, a routine blood test showed a possible increase in tumor activity, and x-rays showed tumors in both lungs. We went to a family reunion in the Midwest with that knowledge, but the doctors said another couple of weeks delay in starting chemotherapy would not matter. The first two types of chemotherapy attempted had no effect on her cancer, and, just after Christmas 1995, she complained of a severe headache, and by the time we got her to the hospital, she was noticeably becoming comatose. She had a 5cm tumor in her brain at the lower rear area. She was given shots to reduce the swelling and was released the next day to proceed directly to radiation therapy. More tumors were found in the back and hip. All except the lung tumors were treated with radiation, and the chemotherapy was shifted to Taxol.

She recovered dramatically, with some weakness in walking and a lot of fatigue, and the monthly x-rays and the blood tests showed a dramatic lowering of cancer activity and all the tumors were shrinking in size. We were exultant. After a couple of months, she began to resume a fair amount of her normal daily activities.

But in the summer, she began to lose some mental keenness. It was generally not noticeable, but if I asked her a question with an "or" in it, she had trouble. If asked, "Do you want pineapple juice?" she would promptly answer yes or no; and answer just as quickly if asked, "Do you want orange juice?" But when asked, "Do you want pineapple juice or orange juice?" there would be this very long pause before I got an answer, and, more and more often, there was this puzzled look as if I had suddenly started speaking a strange language. And she began to walk with a kind of shuffle. We went in for another Taxol treatment and after observing her leg weakness, the oncologist delayed the next treatment for a couple of weeks.

She went downhill very rapidly. She had more and more trouble walking and had trouble getting to the toilet in time before her bladder emptied. Within a few days, she could not walk without help. Calls to the oncologist did not create any apparent concern on his part, and it reached the point where Jean could not walk at all and was demonstrating more and more confusion.

To me, as frightening as anything else was her continued good cheer and total unconcern with her condition except that she hated soiling herself. When I demanded that the oncologist see her, he refused and suggested Hospice. This made no sense to me since at her last visit, he had been all good cheer and hopefulness. He got shouted at and finally agreed to see her if I would bring her in. When I pointed out that I didn't think I could carry her, I was pretty much told that was my problem. The shouting got fairly nasty, and he finally ordered an ambulance and had her admitted to the emergency room. Didn't want to admit her himself.

In the emergency room, the doctor asked Jean why she was there. She smiled her most charming smile at him and said, "I don't know"—and turning to me she asked with great curiosity, "Why am I here?" And now I'm crying as I write this.

Well, she didn't know what year it was, or who was President, etc, and I pointed out that her feet were arched with the toes pointed down. Eventually, she was admitted for a neurology and oncology consult. The oncologist wanted her out of the hospital, but since the x-rays showed her brain tumor had shrunken greatly and her other tumors had shrunk as well, he had some difficulty in explaining that her mental difficulties were the result of cancer activity in her brain. He did keep saying that she was not—in his opinion— treatable. But a request for a diagnosis produced long silences. And without a diagnosis, how does one say she is not treatable? Enter the neurologist, a large man who reminded me of Major Winchester on *M.A.S.H.*, with all the pomposity and none of the charm. Eventually, after spinal taps, MRI, a CAT scan, and various blood tests, we got a diagnosis: Leukoencephalopathy, but I don't guarantee the spelling. Exactly what that was or what her prognosis was (except incurably fatal) was not made clear. What was made clear was that now that they had a diagnosis, she had to leave the hospital. A certain amount of screaming got me an extra day, and we (two of my daughters, actually) turned our living room into a sick room with frantic haste.

And so she came home to die. Her mental deterioration grew markedly from day to day, and it was very difficult to hold any kind of conversation with her. For a few days, she could feed herself with some help, but she could not move her legs. To prevent bedsores, she had to be turned from side to side every two hours during the day and every four hours at night. She had to wear disposable diapers and was incontinent. She had to be bathed and shampooed and lotioned and powdered and massaged, and three times a day get some stretching to prevent her joints from stiffening. She had to have her teeth brushed and flossed, and for some weeks, we put on a little makeup. Personally, I thought of her disease as a sort of combination of Lou Gehrig's disease and Alzheimer's.

I was not totally incapable of taking care of her by myself, but I would have collapsed within a week and resident daughter within two. Jean received superb care because of her daughters, my siblings, our church, and friends. For months, I had one brother and wife or another staying with us; every weekend, my sister and her husband came down from Corona; every weekend, one or more daughters arrived, and the church not only provided spiritual support but lots of visitors for Jean (and she greatly enjoyed visitors even when she couldn't talk to them). For months, we never had to cook a dinner, and for months more, did not have to cook on weekends. That was one great blessing. On many, many days, I was more a personnel and logistics manager than a caregiver. And the logistics could be ferocious.

Another great blessing was the lack of pain. She hurt three times that I can recall: she became constipated, and fixing that really hurt; she got a severe case of diaper rash which was cured in about 48 hours, but it was agony to her each time she had to be cleaned; and once while flexing her wrists, I went too far and she yelled. The last great blessing was her mental deterioration, which seemed first to deprive her of any fear or concern about herself.

She came home at the last of June, I think, and we were told she would not live until September, probably. In September, we were told she could not live until Halloween and at Halloween, that she could not live until Thanksgiving, and then, that she could not live until Christmas.

But she had more and more difficulty eating and then could not swallow fluids. Everything had to be thickened or thinned to the right consistency so that she could swallow it, and it became more and more of an ordeal to get her to take fluids.

Eventually, the day arrived when she could not swallow anything. She had not spoken for weeks; she no longer responded to touch or to sound, but her eyes would blink if I waved my hand right in front of her face. We kept talking to her, but we did not know if she heard or, if she heard, whether she understood.

She died December 29, 1996, at the age of 64. She died in the last hours of the night, before morning came. She died with three of her four daughters and me around her, holding her hands and each others, reading the last rites from the Book of Common Prayer. Her daughters washed and dressed her. Her body was cremated as she desired, and her ashes are in Point Loma Cemetery overlooking the Pacific Ocean.

She, who was always so careful with her life, is dead, and I who was always so careless with mine, live on, trying to do something which in my worst nightmares I never imagined I would have to do: build a life without her. ❖

**Vincent J Felitti, MD,** has been with the Southern California Permanente Medical Group since its opening in the late 1960s. Educated at Dartmouth College and Johns Hopkins, he practiced many years both as a traditional internist and an infectious disease consultant and was an elected Director of SCPMG for ten years.

## Journal Entry, June 14, 2000

*Meditation: "How we spend our days is, of course, how we spend our lives."*
*—An American Childhood, Annie Dillard, 1987*

*How do we make room for spirit in our patients and in ourselves? Whether we call it faith, or instilling hope, or … there is much in healing that is beyond logic, beyond our medications, beyond our procedures … not instead of these things but aligned with them.*

*What is it that the patient and the family bring to the table? What do we, by the gift of ourselves, bring? It is not only our knowledge and our experience as a physician, not even just our compassion … The gift we also bring is in being there, present and whole: mind, body, and spirit, walking with the patient.*

*"Being present" is too easy to forget in the ordinariness of one more patient in one more long day … and in the forgetting, and in the fatigue, we sometimes settle for the mechanical … then we lose our own meaning … the source of our own joy.*

*As people, it is the "ordinary" in our days that soothes and heals each one of us. When we experience a loved one in danger, it becomes so clear in that moment what is important … The background noise fades and we pray for just an "ordinary day."*

*"From the hands of God to our hands …" I don't remember where those words come from, but I know as a physician that is what we are given in our daily work …*

See page 28 for more information about **Kitty Evers, MD.**

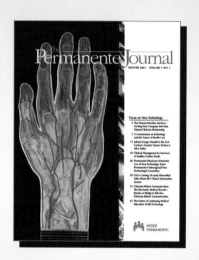

WINTER 2001

*be healer*

An outline of
my own hand,
this hand is
uniquely mine
and yet universal
to all of us.

**Right Hand**
acrylic on bristol board

Inspired by cave paintings in
Europe and Native American
pictographs, this painting
attempts to portray human
hands as icons, decoratively
and anatomically.

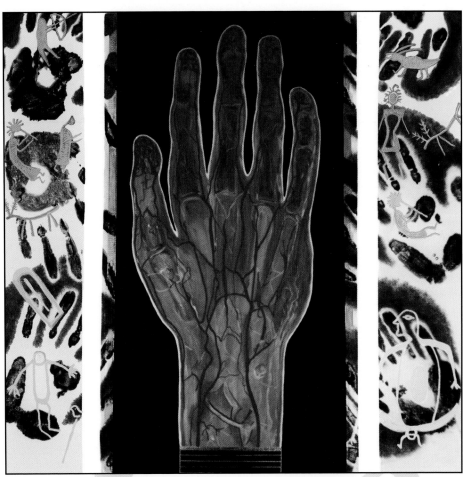

*soul of t*

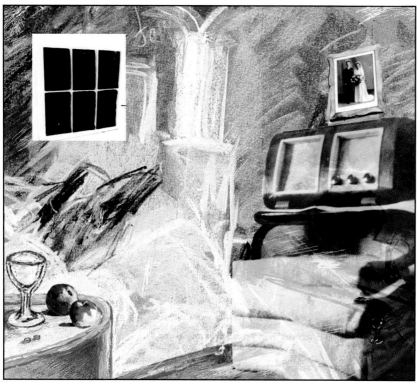

**Still Life**
digital image

## Still Life

The curtains are closed. The room
smells of chrysanthemums
and baby powder. A wet sheet
pastes itself to the bed, drying
slowly in faint brown rings.
The commode is overturned.
Morphine tablets lie
deliquescing
beside an empty glass.
Someone knew he was
not coming back, unplugged
the TV and left.

*Previously published "Spindrift" 2000*

More information about
**Sharon Carter, MD,** can
be found on page 42.

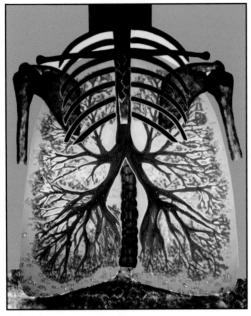

**When it Hurts to Breathe**
mixed media
(acrylics, glass chips, engraved aluminum)

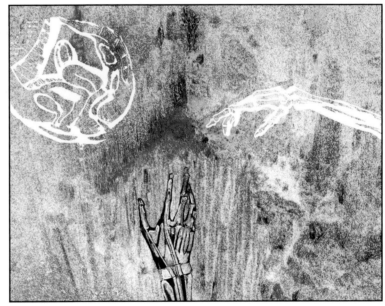

**Wound**
digital image

More information about
**Sharon Carter, MD,** can be
found on page 42.

# A Doctor's Dream

I suddenly long
to be the ennui
musician playing
piano for the
elevator hit
parade in my
left ear as
I wait on
hold to answer
a page while
on call for
another tragic
case of human
misery and despair.

Will my dream
snowball or
fall like a
dried leaf eaten
by a tethered
old goat in
a dank field of
briars and thistle?
Or will it
vanish like the
failed aspirations
of that benumbed
music wizard's
lost youth
spent rehearsing
for my tiny
*otic concert hall?*

**Robert Hippen, MD,** has been a Northwest Permanente radiologist at the Skyline Clinic in Salem since 1991. In addition to poetry, he enjoys music, keeping fit, camping, traveling, spending quality time with his young son and friends, and learning something new everyday.

The
Permanente Journal

SPRING 2001    VOLUME 5 NO. 2

The James A Vohs Award

2  370 Reader Survey Results

11  Introduction

Vohs Award Winner

13  Southern California Heart
Los Angeles Sickle Cell
Medical Care Program

Honorable Mention

20  The Kaiser Permanente
Therapy Management
Strategy (KPTMS)

*Visit us on the Web at:*
www.kp.org/permanentejournal

KAISER
PERMANENTE.

SPRING 2001

*soul of t*

**Beau**

sculpture made of terracotta

"Beau" measures 16 inches high.

**Harry Shragg, MD,** joined Southern California Permanente Medical Group at Harbor City, in 1957, as a general surgeon. He became Associate Medical Director in 1964, and, in 1968, he transferred to West LA to help organize the new medical center and remained there until 1989, then worked part-time in Surgery until 1993. He is now fully retired and living in Brentwood, CA.

**Sondra**

sculpture made of terracotta

"Sondra" is a female nude that measures 15 inches high, 9 inches wide and 9 inches at the base.

## KELLY SIEVERS, CRNA

## The Body Fable

A girl comes to our sterile cell bearing
nameless snakes on the muscle of an arm,
the rise of her ankle. A jewel blooms
in her navel. When we see the red flush
of her tattooed heart we all want to
touch it. Want to ruffle the plume of
purple that flowers above one breast.

She needs us, surgery, a plucking
of her torment. The surgeon toils
in a small wound avoiding a crown
of blackberry thorns. What light did she
lie beneath for a pen to green this vine
across her hip? We are lured, lost
in the feathered uncurlings of her leaves.

I remember when 'Desire me'
was a weedy plague I hid within me.
Unfurled, invisible. I looked for
my reflection in every face on the
street. What could they see?

My fingers flutter above gold rings
piercing this girl's eyebrows. I look
into pinpoint pupils. She ticks in darkness
in the garden of her body.

## Late August

Sycamores are first to curl
and drop their leaves and "I sense"
dry, late August with relief:
the spot on my mother's lung
is not cancer, just an idle
shadow slumbering. I welcome
dormancy, but set sprinklers
in my yard, watering burnt
hydrangea, crisp clematis.

Everywhere I look the world
is withering on spindly legs.
At work a patient recoils
when I touch her arm, "I will
take care of you," I tell her.
"Take care. Take care,"
she repeats. I give her
oxygen, parcelled doses
of anesthesia, unfurl her
twisted legs. Another patient
fingers a St. Teresa medal
pinned to her gown. When I ask
about daughters, she searches
trees outside the window
for ages, names.

In the market
a man cradles his
arthritic hand around a
peach. "Do they feel ripe?"
he asks. I find him
three perfect peaches.

*Previously published in FIREWEED,
Vol 11, No. 3, Spring 2000*

# Biopsy

She wants to know what time it is.
Did she sleep? She has no
time to lose in sleep since probing
fingers circling felt it nestled

jewel-like, beneath her nipple.
A steamy mirror, one arm lifted,
stillness before words rose:
How much time? She needs to know.

Buttoning blouses, moving boxes,
turning toward her lover in
and out of bed, she feared it spoke
to all her cells in secret code
each hour, every stolen minute.

**Kelly Sievers, CRNA,** has been a nurse
anesthetist with Kaiser Permanente since 1982.
Now a part-time employee, she serves as an
associate editor for the literary journal, *The
Grove Review*, and as a reviewer for *The
Permanente Journal's* "Soul of the Healer." Her
work is forthcoming in *The Poetry of Nursing,
Poems and Commentaries of Leading Nurse
Poets*, Kent State University, 2005. She has
been writing poetry and fiction since 1986.

# Maternity Ward

When the sister reads Morning Prayer
over the loud speaker – a Psalm about
seeking light in darkness – I bow my head
and wonder if such prayer is ample
for what we do here.

I am the one who palpates
bones in women's backs, listens
as they pray to break open,
end the pain. *Don't move,*
I tell them as they sway
with fear. *Don't move,* as I slide
thick blunt needles into their backs.

In rooms crowded
with fetal monitors, IV poles,
rocking chairs, husbands, mothers,
aunts, and sisters, I say,
*Breathe slow now,*
my thumb tapping the plunger,
sweat gathering between my breasts,
in the creases behind my knees.

When, in early morning darkness,
I hear them count for ten fingers,
ten toes, I celebrate
this strength to come together
and split apart, this fusion
of fear to joy.

# Nandini Bakshi, MD

IN MY SPARE TIME,
I LIKE TO TRAVEL,
READ AND PAINT.

**10 Degrees South**
photograph
This photo was taken at
Nusa Lembongan, a tiny
island off Bali, Indonesia.

**Clay Pots**
photograph
This photo was taken on a
street in Jakarta, Indonesia.

**Nandini Bakshi, MD,** is a physician in the
Neurology Department with The Permanente
Medical Group in Oakland, CA. She is also on
the teaching faculty as Associate Clinical
Professor of Neurology at UC Davis Medical
Center. She serves on the Oakland Medical
Ethics Committee and the Oakland
Physicians Wellness Committee.

*soul of t*

SUMMER 2001

*e healer*

# ROLAND TCHENG, MD

PHOTOGRAPHY
FORCES ME TO LOOK
MORE CAREFULLY,
TO SEE MORE CLEARLY,
TO SEARCH FOR
PATTERNS AND
CONTRASTING
ELEMFNTS ... ALL OF
WHICH I PRACTICE
EVERY TIME I EXAMINE
A PATIENT.

**Miniature Waterfall**
photograph

*soul of t*

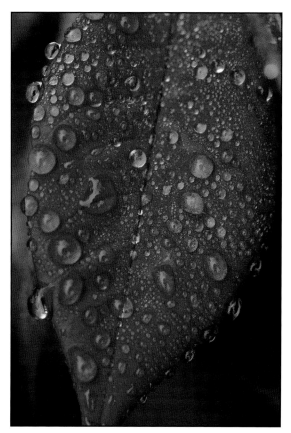

**Raindrops on Red Poinsettia**
photograph

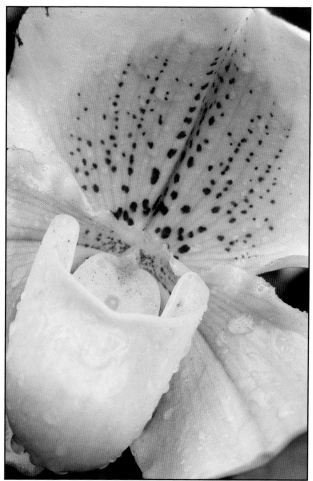

**Yellow Orchid**
photograph

**Roland Tcheng, MD,** has been a dermatologist with the Southern California Permanente Medical Group for 12 years and has been making photographs longer than he has been a physician. "Photography appeals to me for the same reasons I enjoy medicine," says Dr. Tcheng. "There is a science and an art component to both. One can master the science and technicalities of controlling the camera, lens, and film, but without interacting with the subject and light in a personal, human way, the photographer will fail. The same can be said for succeeding in medicine and helping patients."

## Anatomy Lab

His name was Luther,
at least, that is
what we called him.
We chose him
because he was
slender and lay
next to an
open window.
Why did he donate
himself to our
awkward probing,
the sophomoric pranks?
Or didn't he know?
His body was
our textbook.
Was he a loner,
or did he have
family? Did he
work with his
hands, or languish

in prison or asylum?
Was he loved?
What were his longings?
We never even knew
how he died.
As in slumber
he lay, object
of our novice
trespass, and
with dignity bore
his defacement.
Forgive us,
dear father,
reform your
unenlightened
sons and daughters.
Hear us now,
famous warrior,
with those lifeless
ears, with sightless

eyes, see us in
the miasma of our
mid-life careers.
We know now
your sacrifice
cannot be repaid.
Your formaldehyde-
soaked fingers
will forever linger
in our minds,
as we administer
your teachings
to the dying
and the damned.
How well you
taught your
children, in
the anatomy
lab of memory.

— January 25, 2001

More information about
**Robert Hippen, MD,** can
be found on page 81.

**Worry Man**

line art

This sketch is based on Don Wissusik's experiences while stationed at a small US Air Force medical clinic in the Mediterranean during the mid 1970s. During his duty stay, he experienced terrorist attacks, political turmoil and war between Greece and Turkey. The drawing sums up his emotional journey through the life events that he witnessed during that period.

**Don Wissusik, MA, MS,** is a Clinical Services Manager for the Department of Addiction Medicine at the KP Tualatin, Beaverton, and Sunset Clinics in Oregon.

# CAROL NELSON

I ENJOY CREATING PRIMARILY
COLORADO LANDSCAPES AND
FLORALS IN WATERCOLORS, OILS,
ACRYLICS, AND COLLAGE.

**High Country September**
oil

**Denver Sunset**
watercolor

**Carol Nelson** is a medical technologist at the Kaiser Permanente Regional Reference Hematology Lab in Denver, CO. She is very involved in the Denver art community. More of her artwork can be viewed on her Web site: www.art.com/ memberartist/Carol_D_Nelson.

*soul of t*

FALL 2001

*be healer*

THIS IMAGE
IS MAGICAL.
THE EXPERIENCE
WAS RELIGIOUS.

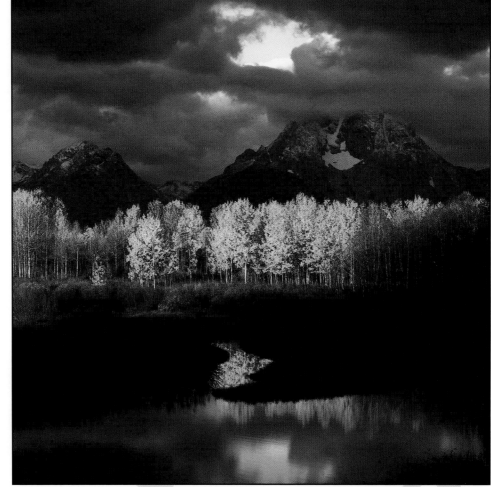

**Sunrise at
Oxbow Bend**

photograph

This image was captured
in October at Oxbow
Bend in the Grand Teton
National Park, Wyoming.
Dr. Mittleman woke an
hour before sunrise to
wait until well past
sunrise in the dark, cold,
and rain. As he was about
to "pack it in," there was a
break in the clouds. The
sun, well above the
horizon, illuminated the
row of Aspen trees.

*soul of t*

**American Avocet**

photograph

This image was captured at the Bear River Migratory Bird Refuge in Brigham City, UT. This bird is in breeding plumage. The early morning light makes the image warm and golden. When not in breeding plumage, the Avocet's head is gray and the black color on the body becomes gray.

**Lesser Scaup**

photograph

This image was captured on Coronado Island, CA. The reason for making this image was not the bird, but the reflections of color in the water. The color reflections are from kayaks that were stacked near the water. There was just a brief period of time when the sun was in the right position to cause this effect.

*All the bird images are of free and wild birds. Many extraordinary wildlife images seen in publications today are captive animals in settings that make them appear to be wild.*

### Black Skimmer
photograph

This image was made at the San Joaquin Sanctuary in Irvine, CA. The Black Skimmer is the only bird whose lower bill is longer than the upper. It skims over the water with the longer, lower bill feeling for fish. This image is backlit, which gives it a unique feel.

### Brown Pelican
photograph

This image was made on the cliffs at La Jolla, CA. When not in breeding plumage Brown Pelicans are just that, pretty much brown. This bird is in prime breeding plumage with the sky blue eye (eye color often changes when a bird is in breeding plumage), red throat pouch and yellow head.

**Richard Mittleman, MD,** has been a pediatrician with the Southern California Permanente Medical Group for over 25 years. He has had images published in Birder's World Magazine, had an image selected in the Pfizer Calendar contest, and exhibited work at the last annual Pediatric Education Conference. More of his work can be viewed at: www.gon2foto.com.

THE HUMERUS ZONE

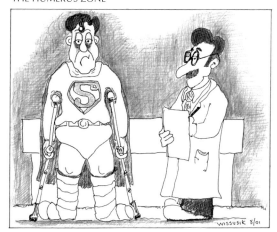

You may be the man of steel, but at your age, NO MORE leaping tall buildings in a single bound!

THE HUMERUS ZONE

Now Mr. Adams, what seems to be the problem?

See page 91 for more information
about **Don Wissusik, MA, MS.**

**Traffic Circle, Budapest**

photograph

See page 12 for
more information
about **Stu Levy, MD.**

*soul of t*

## Stress

A definition, friends, of stress:
Your own reaction to a mess
Stresses may be large or small
Sometimes they're not perceived at all
Examples: Say a lack of cash;
A just-avoided freeway crash;
An allergen that's in the air;
The barber says you're losing hair;
Fifty on a spavined horse;
Attorney's letter *re* divorce;
Wetness, dryness, heat or cold;
Callow youth or getting old
Stress from pains to pleasures range
The common element is *change*
Adapt or die, and that's a fact
And so our bodies must react:
The heart speeds up, the gut slows down

Facial muscles snarl or frown
Bronchial tubes expand and then
The blood absorbs more oxygen
Widened pupils search the void
Adrenal glands secrete steroid
Serum glucose starts to climb
More insulin works overtime
Stressed physically or mentally
Muscles tense to fight or flee
The midbrain boils with rage and fear
While cortex plans to save your rear
The point is, stress is not unique
It doesn't mean you're dumb or weak
A part of mankind's constitution
Bequeathed to us by evolution
Common both to man and beast
It proves you're still alive, at least.

**William Goldsmith, MD,** is a psychiatrist at the Kaiser Permanente Medical Center, Lancaster, CA. He has a Bachelor of Arts in English. He is a veteran of Vietnam and Desert Storm and, in 2004, was deployed as a flight surgeon with the 708th Air Expeditionary Group. He flew on combat and support missions to Afghanistan, Pakistan, and Kyrgystan. Dr. Goldsmith regretfully retired from the Air National Guard in December 2004. He is married and has two sons.

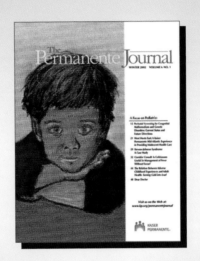

WINTER 2002

*soul of t*

**Zoe**
pastel

"Teo" is a pastel portrait of Dr. Smith's son. This pastel, along with "Zoe," her daughter were drawn five years ago. These were her first creations using pastels.

**Teo**
pastel

I LOVE THE CREATIVE PROCESS IN MANY MEDIUMS, BUT PLASTIC SURGERY IS WHERE THE CULMINATION OF MY DISPARATE INTERESTS AND TALENTS ALLOW THEIR BEST AND MOST IMPORTANT EXPRESSION.

**Tina M Smith, MD,** is a plastic surgeon for The Permanente Medical Group. She trained at Stanford, and immediately following training, she took Dr. Robert Pearl's advice and joined TPMG.

**"Canyon Vistas"**
watercolor and pastels
This is a landscape overlooking the Mission Valley of San Diego.

**Lis MacDonald, NP,** formerly a primary care nurse with the Southern California Permanente Medical Group at the Point Loma Clinic in San Diego, CA, began painting watercolors about nine years ago and enjoys painting landscapes and portraits.

My subjects have varied over the years and include travel photography, landscapes from afar and close up, people, and professional topics in my work.

**"Snowbound"**
photograph
This photo was taken from the window of Dr. Fremland's boyhood home, in St Paul, MN. He used a Rolleicord camera he purchased with money earned from shoveling sidewalks.

**Alan D Fremland, MD,** was a radiologist with the Southern California Permanente Medical Group in San Diego for 22 years. Upon retiring, he and his wife have traveled for the past ten years, mostly by RV, and resettled in the Hill Country of South Texas, outside of San Antonio. Dr. Fremland has recently been exploring the use of his computer, scanner, and printer instead of a darkroom to produce prints.

## No Flies on Ray Kay

I AM HONORED THAT
THIS POEM WAS READ,
IN 1995, AT
DR. RAY KAY'S FUNERAL
FOLLOWING HIS DEATH
AT 93 YEARS OF AGE.

Ray Kay, a giant of health
fits in a small chair
sits low behind the table,
has the presence of an enormous stone
high on the rimrock.

A fly, no eagle, dives for his head
smooth for a soft landing,
as Ray explains how,
to a like group with wonder,
he started on a dream
against great resistance
but with patience and persistence.
Ray shifts mid-sentence,
the fly misses, dives again,
shift, miss.
Dive, shift, miss.
Ray, at 89, smiles softly,
he's faster than a fly.

The fly dives buzzing in his ear
nearly crashing in a tuft.
Ray swipes his hand before his face
muffling words about Sid and Irv.
Ray, so mildly annoyed
but with a large smile of new purpose says,
"I'm going to kill that damn fly!
If I can catch him."
Dive fly.
Swipe, swipe!

Ray dislodges his hearing aid,
now perched and teetering.
Disabled, he can't hear the buzz.
"Get the mic back, Irv.
I'll smack it!"

Ray readdresses the group
and chuckles undisturbed.
"Have to say I liked Henry Kaiser
though he took his shoes off."

After terrorizing the front row
of dutiful students,
the fly dives for Ray.
Ray shifts and smiles, says,
"He sure loves me
doesn't he.
That fly's going to feel bad
when we finish here."

Ray ends,
the crowd roars!
Ray Kay smiles triumphantly.

No fly
ever landed
on our Ray Kay.

*This poem was inspired at the 1991 Southern California Middle Management
Development Program, where the physician and manager students listened to Dr. Kay
recount Kaiser Permanente history as a fly buzzed about his head. He showed us
then, as he had in the past, the persistence of greatness in the face of adversity—
a message to help us now as health care changes. While this poem is on the lighter
side, it attempts to capture, by contrast, the brilliance of Dr. Kay.*

**Tom Janisse, MD,** is an anesthesiologist
and Editor-in-Chief of *The Permanente
Journal* in the Northwest Region. More
information about Dr. Janisse can be
found on page 137.

**At The Refugee Campus**
acrylic

See page 59 for more
information about
**Mohamed Osman, MD.**

The
Permanente Journal

SPRING 2002    VOLUME 6 · NO.2

The James A Vohs Award

14  Pain Management and Chronic
    Disease Self-Management Programs
    Win James A Vohs Awards

Vohs Award Winner—
Multiple-Region Category
15  Chronic Disease Self-Management
    Program: From Development
    to Dissemination

Vohs Award Winner—
Single-Region Category
24  KPNW Integrated Pain
    Management Program

Visit us on the Web at:
www.kp.org/permanentejournal

KAISER
PERMANENTE.

SPRING 2002

soul of t

DRAWING AND
PAINTING HAVE
BEEN A PART OF
MY LIFE AS LONG
AS I CAN RECALL.

**Blake Gardens**
watercolor
This painting was done
on location in the
gardens at the Blake
Estate in Kensington, CA,
which is now the official
residence of the President
of the Regents of the
University of California.

**Martinez Waterfront**
watercolor
Martinez is a small
community on the
Northern San Francisco
Bay. The waterfront
illustrates the contrast of
decaying past and
recent renewal.

**Natalya Nicoloff, NP,** is in the Internal
Medicine Department at the Kaiser
Permanente Medical Center in Hayward, CA.
Ms. Nicoloff comes from a family of artists
starting in Macedonia four generations
ago. She is fascinated with the interaction
of water and color. When she is not
working, she can be found painting
watercolors, studying Flamenco dance
and Aquatic Master's swimming.

JOHN H COCHRAN, JR, MD

# A Reflection

Arrogance is the wayward twin of Confidence.

Arrogance is self-promoting and needy;
Confidence is humble and secure.

Arrogance is noisy yet weak;
Confidence is quiet yet strong.

Arrogance tries to be interesting;
Confidence seeks to be interested.

**John H Cochran, Jr, MD,**
is the Executive Medical
Director and President of
the Colorado Permanente
Medical Group for Kaiser
Permanente.

*soul of t*

I HAVE ALWAYS CHALLENGED MYSELF TO TAKE A BLANK PIECE OF PAPER AND USE IT TO EXPRESS EMOTIONS AND FEELINGS THAT ARE NOT EASY TO PLACE INTO WORDS.

**Vanessa**
graphite drawing
The artist, Don Wissusik, MA, MS, completed this drawing when he was a young art student.

See page 91 for more information about **Don Wissusik, MA, MS.**

# ANNA MARIE AGUIAR

I ENJOY PAINTING
FLOWERS BECAUSE
THEY TRANSCEND
EVERYDAY LIFE.

**Flowers in a Copper Vase**

watercolor

This watercolor was inspired by the
simplicity of calla lilies. She contrasted
their soft beauty with the hard, shiny
surface of the copper vase.

**Cloistered**

watercolor

This watercolor was done from a
photograph of the convent in Santa Clara.
Ms. Aguiar chose the subject because it
represents a place of solitude and peace.

**Anna Marie Aguiar** is a
physical therapist assistant
with The Permanente
Medical Group at the Santa
Clara Medical Center.

*soul of t*

THE HUMERUS ZONE

*Don't worry, just a slight medication reaction.*

THE HUMERUS ZONE

*That's good. Now exhale.*

See page 91 for more information
about **Don Wissusik, MA, MS.**

AS A DERMATOLOGIST, I WAS IMPRESSED WITH THE CANADIAN PUBLIC EDUCATION POLICIES REGARDING SUN PROTECTION.

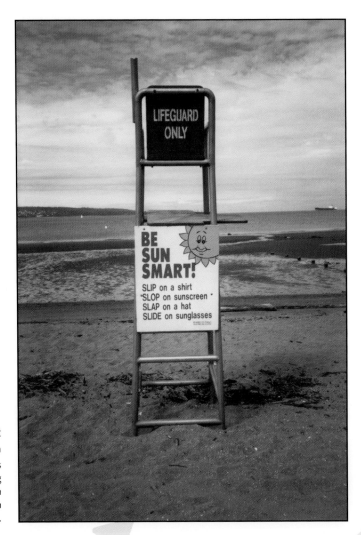

**Be Sun Smart**
photograph
This photo was taken while strolling along the beach in Vancouver, British Columbia, Canada.

**Judith Schiffner, MD,** is a dermatologist at the Fremont Medical Offices in Northern California. She is an amateur photographer, and likes to take photographs during her travels.

SUMMER 2002

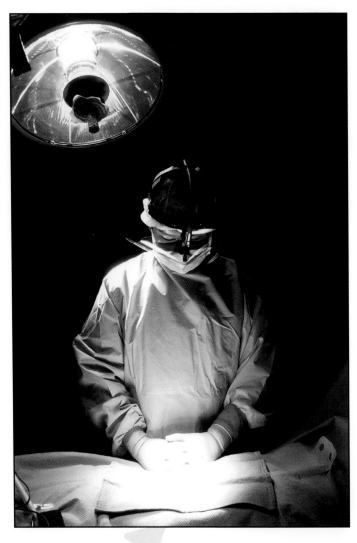

I HOPED TO CAPTURE
THE COMPASSION,
DETERMINATION AND
RESOLVE OF THE
PRACTITIONER IN USUAL
SURROUNDINGS

**Do No Harm …
a Surgeon's Prayer**
digital photograph
An award-winning digital
photograph, taken to honor
the tireless and dedicated
surgeons who love to
practice their art.

**Ninad Dabadghav, MD,** is a general surgeon with
The Permanente Medical Group at the Santa Clara
Medical Office in Northern California. He has
specific interests in surgical oncology and graphic
medical art. Dr. Dabadghav became passionate about
photography when he received a digital camera.

# On Returning to Clinical Practice

I began practicing internal medicine and gastroenterology for the Southern California Permanente Medical Group (SCPMG) in 1969. Over the years, I became interested in medical group management and, in 1989, I left the clinical practice of medicine to take on the role of Area Associate Medical Director for the SCPMG West LA Medical Center. I then had the honor of becoming SCPMG's Regional Medical Director in 1994. Thus, I haven't seen a patient in 13 years.

I'll be retiring as Medical Director at the end of 2003 and am determined to regain some of my medical skills. I have already spent four months at our Inglewood medical offices studying and being proctored. I want to thank Dr. Manny Myers in internal medicine for helping to guide me through this process (ironically, I hired Dr. Myers in 1979 while I was Chief of Medicine at West LA). I'm finding that the medical journals I've skimmed through in the last 13 years haven't prepared me for so many changes—it feels like I've been in outer space. While the interpersonal aspects of medicine have largely stayed the same, the differences in the technical aspects are striking. I would like to describe what I have encountered upon returning to clinical practice.

The nurses, physicians, and staff members are just as wonderful as ever, but now seem *very* respectful toward me (maybe they've realized I sign their checks—hmm …). They also seem a lot younger than they were 13 years ago. In contrast, the patients are definitely older these days, and it's very encouraging to see our members living longer, healthier lives. Wow … the number of things that have to be done to meet the needs of elderly patients! Thank goodness the chief of service is scheduling me lightly until I get up to speed.

Additionally, I now have access to an endless array of systems and technology that simply were not in place before 1989. When I was practicing then, a patient might come in and ask for the results of a cholesterol screening performed the previous week. It would take me up to 20 minutes to find those results—getting the patient's name, calling the lab, finding the chart … Now, all of the information available on the computer makes interactions like this effortless. Online test results, online appointment schedules, e-script, e-referral—all of these technologic advances have made managing the care of patients easier. I am also able to make my progress notes appear erudite by taking information from the Permanente Knowledge Connection (PKC).

I've noticed a reduction in the frustration level of our members as a result of access improvement. In the past, patients would spend the first few minutes of their appointment talking about their difficulties with the phones and how long they had to wait to see somebody. This doesn't happen nearly as much as it did in the '70s and '80s. Of course, members can become frustrated, but the remarkable improvement in access, especially on the phones, is a wonderful accomplishment.

The number of drugs, tests, and therapeutic options available to me are simply awesome. I've had to become familiar with new drugs for diabetes and to choose from countless medications—all while trying to follow the clinical guidelines. And for each patient I've seen, there has always been an additional way to provide care—a test, a medication, a referral—whereas 12 to 15 years ago, I would more often have to tell a patient that there was nothing more to be done. There are fewer instances of that now.

In some respects, I feel as if I never stopped practicing medicine. My techniques of physical examination and diagnostic skills have returned to me easily. Also, I haven't lost my bedside manner—my ability to get close to a patient—something of a surprise after more than a decade of dealing exclusively with physicians, staff, and administrators.

More than anything, I realize that I've been missing out on the fun of interacting with patients. Recently, while examining an 84-year-old patient, I explained to him and his wife that because I was just recently back in practice, another physician would review my work. His wife recognized me because she had been a nurse in the ICU at Kaiser Permanente in the '70s. I appreciated her confidence—as far as she was concerned, I didn't need any help treating her husband. Of course, I can't expect all of my patients to trust me so quickly. But, as always, my demonstration of caring elicits the same level of confidence it did when I was actively practicing medicine. Returning to patient care after being away for so long reminds me how fortunate I am to be a physician.

After more than a decade of working in a leadership role, returning to clinical practice has really made me happy. The array of options has broadened, but the satisfaction that comes with caring for a patient remains the same. It feels so good to begin the journey home. ❖

**Oliver Goldsmith, MD,** was Medical Director and Chairman of the Board of the Southern California Permanente Medical Group, and a member of the Executive Committee of The Permanente Federation. He is now practicing internal medicine and gastroenterology at the Walnut Center Campus.

# KITTY EVERS, MD

## Liberty Park—WTC911

J Seward Johnson's "Double Check"
Bronze business man
Suit covered in ash
Debris everywhere
Briefcase open
Staring down at his waiting work.

He'll never get to that.

Did he know
Death waited instead?
Everything around him transformed
Rendered unrecognizable
In the moment
The sky rained down.

Poor bronze man
You are a stand in
For all of us
That awful day.

You are Everyman's son.
You are Everywoman's child
Still sitting impossibly frozen
Amidst the dust and debris.

Hate leads to this.

What is there left to say?
What is there left to mourn?

No more music
No more sound
Struck dumb
To feel what has come to pass.

And what the poet said is true:

"This is the way the world ends
This is the way the world ends
This is the way the world ends

Not with a bang but a whimper."[a]

[a] The Hollow Men, TS Eliot

*In the aftermath of the bombing of the World Trade Center Towers, many searched for ways to find meaning or solace. Art and poetry became useful expressions of the search. A photograph of J Seward Johnson's sculpture, "Double Check," in Liberty Park, near the World Trade Center, was the inspiration for this painting and poem. In the midst of a normal day, a maelstrom raged around this "Everyman." It is fitting that in the months since the tragedy, this sculpture has become a memorial of sorts, representing those who died in the bombing of the World Trade Center Towers.*

To paint and
to write is
my great joy.

**Butterfly Wings
and Tears**

acrylic

This piece was
painted in response
to a poem Dr. Evers
wrote not long after
the bombing of the
World Trade Towers.

More information about
**Kitty Evers, MD,** can be
found on page 28

RENATE G JUSTIN, MD

## Retire and Practice

The day I retired was grey and gloomy. My mood matched the low clouds and drizzle. I was sad, dispirited. Medicine, with its challenges, frustrations, and joys, had been part of my life for fifty years. Now my ability to give and teach, to comfort and heal, would be terminated. I would no longer be seeing patients, practicing medicine. I was so convinced of this that I even dropped the MD from my name. However, putting my stethoscope in a drawer and giving my white jackets to my grandchildren for their Halloween costumes did not, as I had anticipated, end the practice of family medicine for me. I am still consulted by friends, neighbors, and former patients. They contact me because they are frightened, bewildered, need explanations and my listening ear rather than penicillin or Prozac.

One recent afternoon, a middle-aged gentleman came to my door to thank me for a plant I had sent to him when he was hospitalized for radical prostatectomy. He refuses the coffee I offer but stays an hour and more to tell me about the frustration he is experiencing due to his postop course. He was prepared for incontinence but not for the embarrassment it is causing him. I have little to offer other than empathy and time to allow him to talk about the problem he faces, always having to carry extra clothing, as well as his concern that his colleagues might notice a urine odor. I am surprised at the candor with which he discusses his difficulties since I am only superficially acquainted with him. He is more relaxed when he leaves and tells me that he appreciates the visit in my home more than the plant I gave him. He asks if I would permit him to return to talk again? Undoubtedly he values the fact that, as a retired physician, I have more time to listen to him than his surgeon, who always has other patients waiting. It gives me

> BEFORE RETIREMENT, RECEIVING CALLS ABOUT MINOR AILMENTS WHILE SEEING ANOTHER PATIENT IRRITATED ME; NOW I NO LONGER FEEL RESENTFUL BUT INSTEAD FEEL HONORED ABOUT BEING INTERRUPTED.

satisfaction that, due to my calling, I understand the devastating effects of illness and therefore can still ease the pain of those around me. No family physician is unaware of the powerful healing qualities of quiet listening. When I was first in practice, I had the luxury of using that tool and learned how much is revealed to the silent listener. At the end of my career, it became more difficult to listen adequately due to time constraints. Now that I am retired, I can once again listen attentively for as long as necessary. My visitor realizes this and therefore wants to return.

A former patient's husband calls. His wife, in her late seventies, suffers a sudden onset of confusion and difficulty in speaking. He is unable to contact her primary care physician. I advise him to take her to the emergency room at once. She is admitted to the neurology floor but adamantly refuses to get into bed. At her husband's suggestion, her nurse calls me and tells me that neither she nor the neurology resident can persuade the patient to get undressed. I go to the hospital and have no problem at all helping her to slip off her clothes and get into bed in spite of her confusion. For a moment, I once again enjoy the privilege of practicing medicine, of being in the hospital, of being part of a team—the nurse, the resident, and the patient's husband. By gentle, firm persuasion, I get the patient ready for her brain scan. I feel reassured that I have not lost my touch, used many times in the past, to get an immediate, necessary task accomplished. Fortunately, in a few days the patient's mind clears and she is discharged to her home. She continues to consult me about many discomforts she is experiencing, most of which I can improve with warm water bottles, mild massage administered by her husband, and other benign ministrations. Before retirement, receiving calls about minor ailments while seeing another patient irritated me; now I no longer feel resentful but instead feel honored about being interrupted.

There are also less serious problems about which I am consulted. A head lice epidemic and panic simultaneously strike the middle-class neighborhood in which I live. Out my window I see adults grooming each other, looking for signs of infestation. This epidemic, like many others, wears itself out. Perhaps the experienced voice of the senior member of the community helped to restore calm.

Then comes the phone call from a family who had been patients of mine for 25 years and who now live in a distant town. The parents are desperate because their young daughter has been diagnosed with a rare cancer. I share their concern and worry. A three-year-old child of theirs died many years ago, and I know that the pain of that loss comes to the surface now that they face this potentially fatal illness. They want to know where they should go for care, what is the prognosis, what is the meaning of "nodes lighting up on PET scan"? They are more able, capable, and intelligent than I am and could answer these questions, but they need a familiar, trusted voice to help them through their crisis. Together, we draw up a list of areas they may want to explore with the oncologist. I am sure we will have an ongoing conversation as the cancer reveals its character and we learn how aggressive it is. I think about them often and with deep compassion for their suffering. If our discussion were taking place face-to-face, I would hug the mother and father to express my support for them during the difficult months ahead. I would have a long talk with the daughter about her future, her anxiety. Now I will communicate by letter and telephone and feel humbled by their thanks for my interest. They help me as much as I help them, because I realize now that my fear of not ever being able to use my medical knowledge again to help someone was unfounded.

Many minor injuries come to my house—cuts, nail avulsions, fractured clavicles. Often, the only request is an opinion: Does it need stitches? Do we need to see our doctor or go to the emergency room? Other times, I can apply a bandage, which the youngsters especially appreciate. Somehow knowing that I am a doctor makes the "owie" improve faster than if their mother or father put a Band-Aid® on the wound. When a scraped knee or a minor cut appears at my doorstep, I wish I had a well-equipped office in my home in which I could apply a neat dressing instead of making do with my ill-lit living room, where I worry about bloodstains on the carpet. Obviously, I have to limit myself to listening and advice, and not get involved in treatment, since I no longer carry malpractice insurance. When, over a cup of tea, the discussion turns to the appropriateness of a new prescription, I remain silent and do not comment, even if I have a strong opinion. If asked directly about a medication, I refer the question back to the prescribing doctor.

At times, I am also asked to see injured animals, but there I draw the line. I did that when I practiced in a remote area early in my career, but now I have an acquaintance who is a retired veterinarian, and I refer to him.

Retirement, fortunately, has not eliminated my occasional involvement with patients. Compassion did not dry up when I cleaned out my desk and put the *PDR* next to Shakespeare on my bookshelf. Those who consult me can still benefit from my medical training and experience, and I benefit from knowing that I contribute to someone's well-being. ❖

See page 40 for more information about
**Renate G Justin, MD.**

In a chance meeting we
were drawn to each other

Regretful how little I hear
of your life

Our friendship in the Way
for just a day surpasses ten
years of casual fraternity

— A poem by a Zen monk
Jakushitsu (1290-1367)

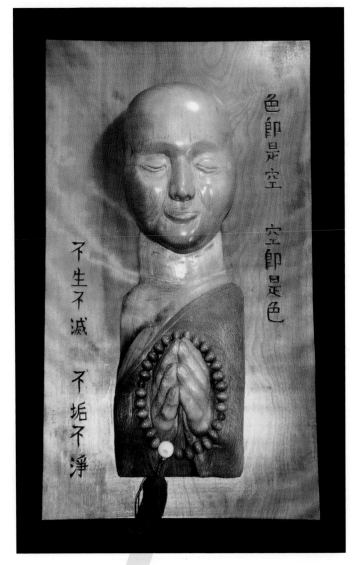

**A Monk Meditating
on Sutra**

woodcarving

This carving, mounted on
alderwood, was created
from a piece of white oak
picked up as firewood.
The Chinese characters are
copied from "The Great
Prajna-Paramita Heart
Sutra," a widely chanted
sutra in the Buddhist
canon. The translation is:
"Shariputra, all things are
essentially empty; not born,
not destroyed; not stained,
not pure; without loss,
without gain."

**Masatoshi Yamanaka, MD,** is
an orthopedic surgeon at the
Skyline Medical Office in
Salem, OR. He is also a
woodcarver and has won blue
ribbons at the Oregon State Fair.

*soul of t*

FALL 2002

*be healer*

# Ahmad Abdalla, MD

**Teardrop Arch**

photograph

A beautiful arch tucked deep in Monument Valley, Utah, far from the eyes of the casual passerby. It required a long desert drive and a short hike for Dr. Abdalla to arrive when the light was perfect for this mid-morning shot.

**A Gathering of Crabs**

photograph

Walking through a fish market on the Potomac, in Washington, DC. Dr. Abdalla was attracted by the orderly arrangement of these crabs.

**Ahmad Abdalla, MD,** joined Southern California Permanente Medical Group in 1978 as a head and neck surgeon. Along with his medical practice, he has developed his lifelong love of photography into a serious profession. He is a graduate of the New York Institute of Photography and is designated as a Master Photographer by the International Freelance Photographers Organization. He has been published repeatedly and his artwork is displayed on many walls in Southern California.

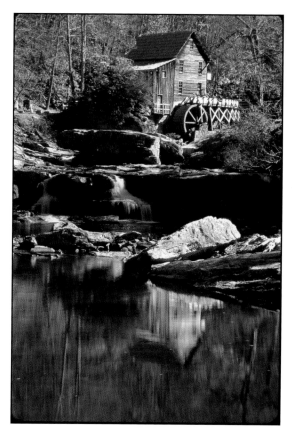

### Glade Creek Grist Mill
### Babcock State Park, West Virginia
photograph

Impressed by a photograph in a magazine three years earlier, Dr. Abdalla's imagination materialized into reality when, on a cold fall morning, he found himself standing in the middle of this beautiful West Virginia setting. Images that had been formulated in his mind over the years had finally been captured on film.

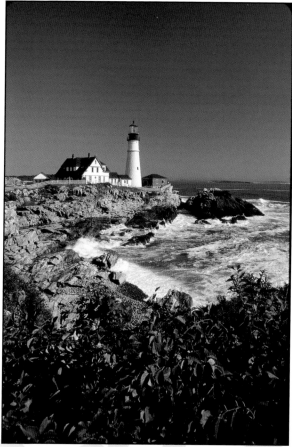

### Portland Head Light
### Portland, Maine
photograph

Born and raised in Alexandria, the city that housed the Pharos lighthouse, Dr. Abdalla says that he has always been attached to lighthouse photography. He has traveled extensively to add to his lighthouse photographic collection. Portland Head lighthouse is one of the most beautiful settings he has come across.

HARD TO BELIEVE THAT
A CHILDHOOD PHOBIA
WOULD BECOME THE
SUBJECT OF MY PASSION.

**Spider Web**
photograph

**Suzanne Ackley, MD,** has been
an orthopedic hand surgeon with
Southern California Permanente
Medical Group in Orange
County, CA since 1986. She lives
in Newport Beach, CA.

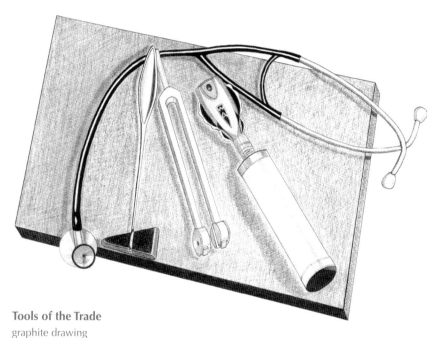

**Tools of the Trade**

graphite drawing

Upon completion of a drawing class, Dr. Kuiper
rendered this 16"x20" drawing of medical equipment
that, with the exception of the newer stethoscope,
served him for 43 years.

**John J Kuiper, MD, FACP,** was an internist
and nephrologist with Southern California
Permanente Medical Group in Panorama
City for 26 years. Since retirement,
he has continued teaching and research
at the UCLA Medical Center.

WINTER 2003

soul of t

THIS IS ONE
OF A SERIES OF
EXPERIMENTATIONS
WITH THE IDEA
THAT PARTICULAR
PAINTINGS CAN
BE VIEWED FROM
DIFFERENT
PERSPECTIVES.

**Primordium**
acrylic on canvas
Dr. Shearn loved bright
colors and odd shapes.
He felt this painting could
be viewed upside down.

**Martin Shearn, MD,** was Chief of Medicine at
Kaiser Permanente Oakland where he developed
the first House Staff Training Program. This
painting was done in 1988, two years after
Dr. Shearn's retirement from The Permanente
Medical Group with 31 years of service.

## Artistic Expression with Dementia

Finally, the words just disappear. Alzheimer's erases them from the brain so completely that the names of mundane objects like "pen" or "watch" cannot be spoken. As his dementia evolved, Dr. Shearn turned from language to painting in order to express himself. With a paintbrush striking against a blank canvas, he stretches a burnished sunset across a sleepy, rugged landscape (page xx). He creates a glossy eye that unflinchingly stares back (page xx). We see sixteen hands—opened, emptied, suspended in motion (page xx), and the primordial beginning of life (page xx).

He speaks in tones of blues and greens and pinks and reds, and he transcribes the internal images with brushstrokes across canvas. He reaches through the fog of his dementia, where the glorious words he had once mastered are obscured, and he connects still, in this inventive way, through this new medium. He continues to do what he has always done as a physician and researcher, venturing beyond the conventional limits of language and medicine to discover and communicate new constructs.

It would be preposterous to pretend knowledge of Dr. Shearn's creative intention or process, impossible to propose an understanding of his art derived from medical theories of disease. Still, much has been written about the relationship between neurocognitive states and artistic expression, and the urge to speculate on that relationship arises here, too. After all, we physicians are consummate diagnosticians who daily seek scientific explanations for our patients' subjective complaints, and we constantly filter those complaints through a focus on pathology. We believe that we can—and even should—discriminate the voice of mind from the voice of body when our patients speak about suffering and distress.

We read medical literature that associates creativity with prefrontal dementias, analyzes Willem deKooning's abstract expressions through the influence of his Alzheimer's dementia, or interprets Ernst Josephson's paintings through his schizophrenia. The new genetics fascinate us and lure us into believing that heredochemical factors might explain our personalities, proclivities, and aesthetics. As physicians, we uniquely wander and wonder about the mysterious nexus between mind and body, health and disease, living and dying.

And still, with every available diagnostic tool in hand, we cannot anatomically locate human creativity. We cannot tell where it resides in our system of propositions for health and disease, our medical notions about personhood and agency. Looking carefully and analytically at artwork created by people in demented or psychotic "states" does not reveal the vast, inscrutable internal worlds in which their creativity originates.

No matter how hard we have examined the human brain, rummaging through thick clumps of tangled neurons or searching under the dark crusts of a thousand cortical scars, we do not know how people create and why they must. Creativity flows from a source of their being that artfully defies our medical investigation and scientific discourse. Creativity humbles us in our quest to become masters of the psyche and body, and it "reminds" us of our astounding incapacity to understand the most rudimentary element of our patients' lives: their exquisite, fundamental aliveness.

I suspect that Dr. Shearn was drawn toward the mystery. I imagine that he ventured purposefully into it, with whatever tools he possessed, to create something new—much as he had always done—in his unique fashion and radical, enduring aliveness. ❖

> LOOKING CAREFULLY AND ANALYTICALLY AT ARTWORK CREATED BY PEOPLE IN DEMENTED OR PSYCHOTIC "STATES" DOES NOT REVEAL THE VAST, INSCRUTABLE INTERNAL WORLDS IN WHICH THEIR CREATIVITY ORIGINATES.

See page 62 for more information about **Kate Scannell, MD.**

**Fishing Camp;
Lake Millinocket, ME**

watercolor

This piece was painted when four medical school buddies had a reunion at a fly fishing camp in Maine. The weather was hot; the water warm; they didn't catch many trout, but had a great time.

**Starry Night;
Basque Series**

oil on canvas

**Paul Ackerman, MD,** is a psychoanalyst practicing in Los Angeles, CA. His son, Douglas Ackerman, MD, is a urologist at the Mt. Talbert Medical Office, in Clackamas, OR. Dr. Ackerman, senior, started painting when he was a teenager and picked it up again four years ago. He paints in oils and watercolors, and works both in realism and abstracts.

# Living with Alzheimer's

We live too long, perhaps. Medicine has performed such miracles in our day, but when an illness such as Alzheimer's strikes, there is little to be done but wait.

Martin and I have been married for over 50 years. We have been partners, filling various roles in each other's lives and in society. Now, however, we have had to adopt new roles.

Who are we? He is a husband, father, grandfather, a physician, an honored teacher, a professor, and a mentor for a generation of rheumatologists. He has written myriad learned articles for the medical literature as well as books and a number of lighthearted, joyous celebrations of special and often-entertaining observations.

I am a wife, mother, grandmother, an immigrant from Hitler's Europe, and a college graduate. I have been the financial officer for the Oakland Symphony, a docent at the California Academy of Science, a counselor for Planned Parenthood, and a speaker for the Holocaust Center. But my new role is that of "caregiver" for my beloved's new role of Alzheimer's patient.

The word "caregiver" feels ambiguous. It does not begin to describe the magical life that Martin and I shared, the adventures we experienced, the occupations and professions we pursued, or the encomiums we earned—together and individually. A caregiver? Surely that cannot be the only thing I am. Being a caregiver is a long, lingering collection of greater and greater burdens. I miss having a life outside of Martin's illness; but more than that, I miss my best friend and confidant. My other friendships and interests have been eroded. The insidious disappearance of my own life is an incalculable loss, and the cost of energy and of strength is truly overwhelming. The emotional drain is never replenished and leaves a vast hole. I know the negative balance must be replenished or this organism will die. Where will the energy come from? I know Martin will not get better, and I must find my way back to some sort of equilibrium.

Martin made his own diagnosis about ten years ago, when he became aware of failures in his memory. Memory had been his proudest gift. Suddenly, he discovered a glitch in this retrieval process, and it was terrifying to him. "Some forgetting happens to everyone as we get older," we said because it felt reassuring.

For him, the first defense was secrecy: No one must know of this "shameful" loss. But a very few were quietly asked for their impressions: Medical friends and doctors who were not friends were invited to do a clinical evaluation. The favorite explanation was "it's definitely not serious; it's pseudodementia and can be cured by an antidepressant. Start today, and in two weeks you will be better." We wanted to believe. He wanted to believe. As soon as the first dose was taken, he was "better" and happier. But, of course, the gains were not sustained. More testing was needed. And more. And more. We finally decided to do complete psychological testing because "he feels so bad about retiring from medicine."

The results pointed to early dementia, and, for the first time, the "A word"

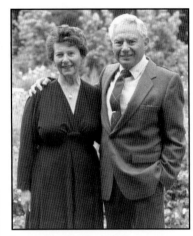

Dr. and Mrs. Shearn, 1998

was mentioned. This prospect was grim, but initially we were able to make adaptive changes in our life. We worked diligently to introduce some new activities: Teaching medicine to laymen, presenting workshops on poetry, and discussing biographies at senior centers. It made us both feel better. But the memory problem was clearly getting worse. He would get angry, even with me—a totally new phenomenon. He didn't want to talk about it. He began living an insular existence.

And then, a fabulous gift was unwrapped. He discovered within himself a passion for painting. He created remarkable images and was lauded by all for the amazing range of his talent and for the beauty of his colors, his composition, and his imagery. The pictures depicted large, fantastic skyscapes of great intensity or nostalgic reminders of another time with life-sized nickelodeons featuring some of the songs of our youth, and ice cream sodas of enormous size, recalling happier days without worries about cholesterol.

Years passed. Martin continued to be athletically active, involved with family matters, and creative. Sadly, his fervent passion for medicine had vanished.

Relentlessly the mental deterioration became more debilitating—clearly more widespread, more pronounced and noticeable. He had ways of coping. While reading, he took notes. When he couldn't understand his notes, he became angry. He blamed others—a distinct change in personality.

We went back for more testing, this time to a research center for Alzheimer's; the deficits were documented. By the end of that visit, we acknowledged the diagnosis we had known for a long time. The certainty required a new attitude. Privately, Martin accepted the diagnosis, but he did not feel comfortable discussing it with anyone. He withdrew from old friends for fear of what they might think. We saw no colleagues, avoided medical meetings, rounds, and most friends; only a few who pursued us succeeded in reaching him.

There were legal issues to be attended to, and Martin clearly expressed his wishes in writing that he did not wish to live if his brain ceased to function. He contemplated a life with greater and greater losses.

My personal loneliness was exacerbated by his unwillingness to discuss our fate with friends or with family. Of course, our children knew, but he didn't want to talk about it with them either. I needed to tell those who love us—our friends and relatives—but he did not want to burden them. Also, I guess, he was embarrassed.

Eventually, my insistence brought us to the Alzheimer's Association, and we joined a support program, but still Martin was not willing to share his feelings. I continued alone and found a most supportive group. Aside from that, we were alone.

When he could no longer make sense of reading, he took a shocking action. He destroyed some favorite books. He snatched them off the shelf, cut the pages into pieces, and threw them away. "There was nothing in them," he said.

And yet, I am not crying out in anguish; nor am I in a state of denial. It is as if I have gotten used to this disease's huge presence in our life. I can remember what we had. We shared the most amazing and satisfying years. The thrills and excitement of our mutual discovery of each other empowered both of us to considerable accomplishments. His thinking was always original, dependable, and multifaceted. He had found it possible to take an idea, turn it upside down, and then state it in a better way. It has given us both so much delight to write articles on subjects that had never been explored before, or to expand studies to give a new slant on an old is-

sue. So, even though Martin's memory is gone, I still have mine. And we have his writings, his files, and his pictures. We often look at our past life in this way. Martin's sense of humor remains, though now more like a child's. Although his words are most often clear, comprehension and meaning are no longer there.

We have been so blessed to be together as we raised our children in a medium of love, intellectual stimulation, and the games of the mind. He was always able to translate his role as a serious teacher of medicine to that of a very playful father, joyfully detailing the perversions and contradictions of humanity in a difficult and cruel world. He inspired our son, David, and daughter, Wendy, to become physicians and both are with The Permanente Medical Group. Our daughter Bobbi became a physical therapist and is now a musician.

Martin has always been compassionate. His patients adored him because he truly searched for the spot in their lives he could understand—to which he could connect. We sometimes reread their letters of appreciation. I knew that his students would remember too. This, then, became a possibility of return to sociability, I felt. Without his permission, I contacted selected former medical residents and suggested that they visit him and that they pass the word around. His diagnosis was no longer a secret.

FATE CAN BE CRUEL, BUT THIS NEW STAGE IS PART OF OUR LIFE—THOUGH NOT TOGETHER IN THE OLD WAY.

It was liberating for me. Martin didn't need to talk about it. Many of his admiring ex-residents came to visit, and he basked in their warmth and friendship. They didn't talk medicine. He was interested in their lives and families. There were lots of laughs. It was a marvelous interlude.

As his cognitive skills continued to decline, his emotional side came more fully to the fore. His love for me is expressed a thousand times a day, though I detect a desperate dependence—every minute, every day, everywhere.

As language skills have diminished, the brain centers of emotion and whatever controls the arts have expanded. He no longer has the ability to paint on his own. Initiative seems to have dried out. But he still loves art, and he now has an art therapist to help him—one-on-one—create newer, simpler pieces. He is rapt with attention as they work, and he enjoys the process and what he creates. He continues to love listening to music and has expressed an earnest desire to play the piano. He can no longer read music, but he can sing and play all the old songs by ear. He can't remember the words. We have a music therapist who works with him, and he thoroughly enjoys that activity.

He now has caretakers—other than me, who come daily, eight hours a day, and he enjoys their attention, nature walks, the birds and flowers that flourish around us—and he chats with all the dogs and babies in the neighborhood. It is heartbreaking for me to note that, instead of conversations with Nobel Prize winners, he now counts or comments on the caw of the crows. He is extremely sociable with all strangers. He is no longer aware of the diagnosis. He feels lucky that he is healthy, and he agonizes over the dilemma of others who have been afflicted by debilitating diseases. He likes to play and to pun and to laugh. He seems incredibly happy most of the time—joyful and sweet and kind.

Our grandchildren are amazingly attuned to his abilities and often involve him in their games. But they are noisy and wild, and he feels excluded when conversation does not center directly on him.

I try to concentrate on the pluses and not the minuses. I will continue to do so. I will not allow myself to wallow—not in despair, not in simple pessimism—at least not very much. My mind works. My children are helpful and kind and near and contribute greatly to my day-to-day comfort and pleasure. My grandchildren are a joy and they too are sweet and kind and near. Perhaps I'll get busy with a new project, or I will write, or I will travel. Somehow I will contribute. My life is not empty. I play the piano. I read. I attend classes. And I address children's classrooms to talk about my Holocaust experience.

Our devoted children are ever-present. Martin seems to know who they are, but maybe he doesn't. They now worry more about their mother's well-being than their dad's. Perhaps we all have to learn to step away a bit more to save ourselves. They have lives of their own, and they must live them. We are beginning to have family gatherings without dad. The first of these, a few months ago, was most traumatic for me. I felt that a new chapter of my life had begun—without my love. Everyone listened when Bobbi, our daughter, played a song on her violin that she had written. It wailed and throbbed with feeling, and it broke the dam of my self-control. I was dissolved in tears, surrounded by my family, who care so deeply about us both. The full impact of my terrible loss engulfed me.

I have benefited enormously from Martin's loving. We have appreciated so much in each other—strength, athleticism, writing ability, giving to others of our own bounty—that it surely has spurred me on to better performance as a person. Fate can be cruel, but this new stage is part of our life—though not together in the old way. We must go forward toward the unknown abyss, and we will both attempt to be pacific. ❖

**Lori Shearn** is the wife of Martin Shearn, MD. She has volunteered with the Oakland Symphony, the California Academy of Science, Planned Parenthood, and currently speaks at the Holocaust Center.

ANOTHER
EXPERIMENT WITH
PICTURES THAT
CAN BE VIEWED
UPSIDE DOWN
OR SIDEWAYS.

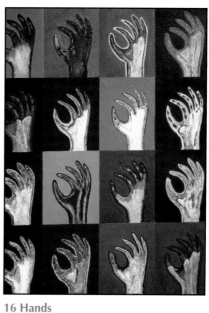

**16 Hands**
acrylic on canvas

This is another in Dr. Shearn's experiments
with pictures that can be viewed upside
down or sideways. He sometimes referred
to this piece as 80 fingers.

**Sunset**
acrylic on canvas

Dr. Shearn's home was high on a hill overlooking
the San Francisco Bay; he could frequently see
spectacular sunsets out of the front window.

For more information about
**Martin Shearn, MD,** see page 127.

# TOM JANISSE, MD

## "You'll Never Get Off the Table"

"Doctor, it's Carla in ER, the Tyler police just called. Medic 3, Tony's rig, is rolling in Code 2 with a suspected leaking abdominal aortic aneurysm. That's what Tony said the patient said. They're twenty minutes out."

"A triple A! Why not Code 3?" said Stewart from the sleep room.

"Patient said not to. Police don't know any more. Tony's probably hoping he can go straight to his mortuary."

"Why are the police calling?"

"You don't know Tony," she said. "He's always hated this medic stuff. In the sixties, back before EMTs, he'd just cruise out to the accident scene in his Cadillac hearse to pick up bodies. Turned on siren and lights to blast through traffic. Not really legal."

"Does he always call the police?" asked Stewart.

"They might have been at the patient's house. Tony calls whoever and whenever he wants, to avoid taking Medic radio orders. He'd still rather go straight to his mortuary than the ER. But doctor … he drives like Mario Andretti!"

"Some story, Carla," Stewart said.

"I'm going on a bit to make sure you're awake. Tony wants to go Code 3 speed, but doesn't want to give Code 3 care. You need to be here when Tony gets here. No telling the patient's condition."

"What time is it?"

"It's 3:15." Carla hung up.

"Thanks," Stewart said to the dial tone.

*Good, not another drunken 19 year old. Wrecked his car. You wonder, when they go off the road on a straight stretch, like last night. Switching tapes? No turns to keep them awake? Unconscious suicide attempt?*

Middle-of-the-night stuff irritated Stewart. A Houston physician, on a research year in residency, he worked in any ER that needed a doctor on the weekend. Tyler County Hospital needed one because the hill town doctors were exhausted seeing patients day and night, in their office, in the hospital, in the ER, quick questions at the flower shop, consultations in the hardware. Even home visits for some old folks.

"Doc, you up? Medic 3 called back. Tony's rounding the corner by the bank. It's Barry Colton. You don't know him but he's got a history of an abdominal aneurysm. Half the town knows. He's 84. Tony says they can't hear the blood pressure now … because of road noise."

"Okay, be there before you can hang up." Stewart slept in his clothes. Gave him an extra minute. He struggled to drag himself out of the deep sleep that he'd fallen back into. His black ruffled hair flowed over his ears and onto his neck. In contrast his mustache was trimmed into a trapezoid. He had an incessantly twitching left upper eyelid. It made him nervous because it meant he was nervous.

*Only August … wish it was 1986 already. Outta residency. Treat a triple A in Tyler? Ship him to Houston before it blows. Not while I'm standing next to him. Vascular surgical team would save him … Tony could take him. Maybe just a kidney stone. A triple A! … in the middle of the night … in Tyler. What a nightmare! Major pain. Like getting shot.*

"Hello, Mr. Barry Colton? I'm Dr. Eddie Stewart. Are you all right? Do you hurt?" Stewart scanned his face and belly for clues. Barry had this eerie look of painful calm on his round face. His ashen hair curled under his ears, matted with sweat against his neck.

"Hurt's here." He pointed mid-abdomen. "Deep. God, it's intense! I gotta have something for pain, doc. I'm dying from the pain."

"Okay, Mr. Colton, but let's see what it is first." Stewart started palpating his belly with his hands one on top of the other, fingers pressed tightly together creating a blunt instrument. "On a one-to-ten scale, how much pain now?"

"Eleven. Christ!"

*Tense, full, yet feeling's distinct. Pulsatile mid-abdominal mass—aneurysm. Belly and back pain—leaking. Hypotension—near rupture.*

"His blood pressure is 70 over 50," Carla said. "Rate's 130." She spoke to him across the bed while plunging the puncture end of the IV line through the soft port in the second bag of saline. As she slid the top slit in the bag over the metal hook, the pole rattled in its base. Carla had a square face, traditional stiff nursing cap pinned on, starched white uniform, nursing pin exactly horizontal on her left lapel. Always adjusting it to make sure.

"Start another large bore line," Stewart said, looking straight into Carla's eyes. "Turn up the oxygen, call EKG, call blood bank for six units, get labs, call Dr. Sovitch, call the OR crew in. Get the floor supervisor down here. And draw up ten of morphine."

"Done." Carla turned to Jimmy, the lab tech who had just run into the room, carrying his basket of color-coded tubes tinkling in little wire cages, and said to him, "You hear those orders?"

"Got 'em. Know the drill from car wrecks." Jimmy pulled out red top, purple top, and green top tubes, a syringe, and tourniquet.

"Mr. Colton," said Stewart, "we're drawing up your pain medicine right now. This looks serious." Stewart, six feet tall, reached down and touched his shoulder. "You know you have an aortic aneurysm?"

"Yes, doc. It's it, isn't it? That's what I told Tony."

"Sure looks like it." Stewart looked up, for the first time noticing Tony leaning against the supply cabinet. He didn't look 60. He was tall and lean with his head down writing his ambulance ticket for the transport down the hill. He wore a navy blue uniform top that zipped up the front. After replacing his call log into his waist pocket, he clicked his ballpoint, twirled it to see the "Hill Country Mortuary" logo on it, then clipped it alongside the log. Tony cured olives every season and brought jars around to everyone he worked with. He even gave Stewart a jar of green ones yesterday. Reminded Stewart of his dad who made little tile trivets and gave them to neighbors. He died last year. Cancer. Stewart felt he should have helped him at the end, as a doctor.

*For all the olives he cures and eats, smoking must dictate his weight. Left his face with creases … visible because he's clean-shaven. Reminds me of a saying, "There are more old lungers than there are old doctors." After smoking ten years … wonder how many lung units I have left? Dad never smoked. Still died.*

"Tony," said Stewart, now over in the corner close enough to talk to him softly, "Can Medic 3 take him to Houston? We can't get a chopper in and outta here in time. They'd have to land up at the airport. Triple transfer."

"Bart's gassin' 'er up now, doc," said Tony. "But doc … don't order CPR in the back. It'd be a flail at high speed. I have two sets of lift tracks in the back. Bart and Barry need to stay on each side for good balance. You know what I'm good at. I can get him to Houston faster than anyone in the county. Cops know the Cad. It's like flyin' a jet under radar. And doc, he doesn't want us doing anything anyway."

"How long?"

"Under 40 minutes with lights 'n siren. The Cad's made for this trip. Cuts through the air like a fish through water."

"Doc, talk to my wife first," Barry interjected, overhearing the exchange. He motioned Stewart over. "Sara should be here. She followed the ambulance in." He paused to take a breath. "I'm not going anywhere 'til you talk to her. She'll tell you what we decided. Hurry doc. This pain is killin' me!"

"His pressure's up," Carla said, "now that we've got some fluid in … 98 over 70."

"Give him the ten of morphine then. Add five if you need to."

Stewart spun around, and took three steps into the hall where he stood along a wall of soft cream tiles across from a tall, slight, 80 year-old woman wearing a long, coat-like, gray woolen sweater. Her reddened eyes emitted tears on a face long in grief, like a window dripping after the rain. A quality of calm accompanied her sadness. "Hello, Mrs. Colton, I'm Dr. Eddie Stewart." The tone of his voice sought resonance with her feelings. "I'm sorry about your husband.

He said you knew what to do." Like the wisp of a wing in flight his fingers touched her forearm.

"Dr. Stewart … it's his aneurysm?" She clutched her small black embroidered purse. She knew but didn't want to.

"Yes, Mrs. Colton."

"Oh dear … we knew it would happen." She blinked, blinked again, then looked down and away, as if searching through the fog for ground.

"We have a plan though, Mrs. Colton," Stewart said, eyelid twitching.

Sara looked around Stewart into the trauma room and saw the people fussing around Barry. She saw Tony. "Is he going somewhere?"

"To Houston. It'll take a team of vascular surgeons to operate on his aneurysm. As a back up, Dr. Sovitch is on his way in. Honestly, even a great general surgeon couldn't save him in Tyler. It's a very complicated operation."

"It's leaking then?"

"I think so, yes, Mrs. Colton."

"Dr. Stewart, he'll never make it through surgery. He's 84, and he's got a bad heart."

"The best thing for his heart could be to fix his aneurysm."

"Dr. Gibon, his family doctor … do you know him?"

"Yes, I met him last month."

"He's Barry's family doctor … always has been. Dr. Gibon told us it was coming; we just didn't know when or where. He said we could either wait and panic or we could prepare and flow with it. After many talks we agreed to no heroics … no tubes." Sara searched for Stewart's reaction.

"We're definitely not there yet, Mrs. Colton, though I'm an emergency doctor."

"Dr. Stewart, I don't want you to be that kind of doctor," said Sara, "I want you to be Barry's doctor." She cupped his elbow in her hand and turned him toward the trauma room, "Let's go in by my husband."

"Hi Barry honey, how are you?" she said, as she grasped his hand in both of hers.

"I'm hurting real bad, Sara. Dr. Gibon didn't talk about this part." Barry looked at Stewart in a plea and said, "Doctor, I gotta get some relief. This is no way to go. Have some compassion for an old man." Barry's face and forehead glistened with beads of sweat. Sara looked at Stewart, then back to Barry.

Carla pressed up against the other rail of the gurney and blotted the sweat over Barry's eyes, then pushed in the last three milligrams of morphine. "That's 15, doctor. I gave it all." She took down the empty bag of saline, replacing it with the unit of blood Jimmy had handed her.

Tony stood by holding the top rail of his shiny tubular aluminum lift with a clean, pressed, white sheet drawn taut and neat around the mattress ready for the transfer. He shifted his weight from one foot to the other. Stewart knew Tony wanted to be rocketing down the road. It's what he got up for in the morning.

Mrs. Colton turned to Stewart, "Dr. Stewart, Dr. Gibon said straight to Barry's face many times in his office, 'You'll never get off the table, Barry, you're too old, and your heart's too sick. If you did survive, you'd suffer a stroke.' Barry wished for the old man's friend—pneumonia—but he's got good lungs. Never smoked."

"I'll never get off this table if I don't get some relief! Give me somethin' more for this pain, please. It's all that matters now."

"Carla, give him another 15 of morphine, please. Carefully. His pressure."

"Hurry, doc! This dyin's hell!"

"Dr. Stewart," said Ginny, one of the OR nurses who'd popped into view in the hall doorway, "we've got the OR ready. All the trauma trays are open, blood's in the OR fridge, and Dr. Sovitch is getting out of his car."

"Thanks," Stewart said, turning back to Sara. "Could I please talk to you for a minute?"

"Yes." She looked to Barry. "We're going to stay together, Barry."

Stewart took her arm and guided her into the hall. "Mrs. Colton, this is very serious. This is life or death."

"Yes, we're ready. Only surprise has been the pain."

"What do you think we should do?" Stewart looked to her imploring for resolution.

"As long as he's comfortable when he goes. That's all that matters."

"Yes, we're doing that. But usually we make every effort. Surgery could save him. We can do that here. Everyone's ready."

"Doctor, he'll never get off the table." She looked annoyed.

"That's easier to say than do," Stewart said.

"Once you took him into the OR I'd never see him again. We planned to be together at the end." She reached for his hand. "Your work now is to relieve his suffering."

"I'll call off surgery then. Tell Dr. Sovitch and the crew. I'll call Dr. Gibon. He'll be awake. We can take good care of Barry right here."

"Thank you." Her face lightened with a faint smile. "Barry said when he passed he'd wait for me. He always does." Looking down and away, like a heron tucking its head in its wing, she stood motionless.

*Dad thought of mom the same way ... when she wanted to give him a pill ... he accepted ... it was the end.*

Stewart's mother was poised at his dad's bedside at home to place a pain pill on his dry tongue, water in hand, saying, "Conrad, here ...."

"Margaret," he responded, "I don't have pain anymore, but I'll do it for you." He swallowed it, and stopped breathing. His eyes widened as if he was seeing beyond, as if he saw friends waiting in the light, drawn to it. He died in that instant. It was a joyous moment, until the reality of death struck her heart.

"His pressure's down to 70 over 40. That's the second unit of blood hanging there, almost in." Carla reached up and squeezed the bag. "We've finished our third liter of saline. And he's got PVCs now. Is it the table ... or the Cad, Dr. Stewart? Table ... or Tony?" Impatient, she wanted action.

Tony caught Stewart's eye and started wheeling over his lift.

Stewart stood silent, arms hung at his sides. His eyelid was still. The green EKG tracing blipped rapidly across the blue screen. Oxygen hissed through the nasal tube. Mr. Colton's eyelids hung heavy leaving only a slit of white. His bulging belly had smoothed out the waves in his gown patterned with turquoise diamonds.

*Duty ... science or heart? Barry wanted it ... Sara did, and Gibon agreed. Never get off ... the table ... or the bed. The table or the bed. Go ... no, not you, it's about Barry ... at peace with death ... but with pain? ... hope now. Dad said, "This is no way to live," before I knew he'd decided ... slipped off ... I was already gone ... planning on Christmas together. Sara's here, Barry's here. Their town hospital ... and Gibon ... their friend too ... right here. I'm in the way. Losing him. Not sure ... morphine knocks out breathing. Advanced age ... pouring in fluid ... heart failure. Hope he doesn't arrest in the ER. Reflex reaction to V Fib near impossible to suppress ... a circus. Jump on him, thump his chest, press his sternum, slap on a mask and pump the bag. A wild primitive dance to restore life. What it would take now. Easy to say, "Do nothing" .... Not sure we relieved pain, or oversedated. Either way, it's good. Sometimes best we can do ... technical training, how's it help? Breathing's slowing. Don't stop breathing here, Barry.*

Stewart suddenly saw Tony across from him. Tony held his lift's side rail behind him with his left hand; his right hand floated above Barry's rail. Stewart called Tony off with a slight wave of his hand and shook his head back and forth several times messaging a no go.

"Let's get him down to his room," Stewart said to Tony, Carla, and Jimmy, all still anticipating action. "Come on, let's go. We're admitting him to treat his pain."

"Doctor," Carla said, while snapping the wheel lock with her foot, "I haven't notified the floor yet."

"Call ahead and find an empty room," said Stewart. "I'll take him and Mrs. Colton."

Finally got him in bed … only a slight grimace.

They were in a single room at the end of the wing that looks out over the hillside through the oaks to the pines up on the ridge. Private. Peaceful. Daybreak. No nursing station calls. "Mrs. Colton, here, let's pull this chair up for you alongside his bed. He looks comfortable now. Resting." She sat on the edge of the chair leaning toward Barry as if looking for signs of distress to relieve, and cupped his hand with her hands.

*God, he's snoring! Sounds awful. Could lead to an obstructed airway … struggling breaths … long, drawing … pulling for air … could just stop breathing trying … then a guttural release of air. Such noises. Quietly … has to go quietly … best for her.*

"Hand me an oral airway please," Stewart requested Betty, the floor nurse now at bedside.

"Number four alright?" she asked.

"Yes, thanks."

"Betty, I'm so glad you're here," said Sara. "We've known you since you were seven. Knew your mom."

Betty smiled. Offered her presence.

*It worked … tongue up … obstruction's gone. Breathing quietly. So undignified, that square plastic protrusion from his dry lips. Could gag him. If terminal gasps, even more pleasant. Guess this airway's better.*

"I'm sorry, Mrs. Colton. I wish we could do more."

"It's all right, doctor." She turned to Stewart long enough for a meaningful connection. "You did the right thing." Sara slid a hand out from Barry's to touch Stewart's.

*Warm, firm grasp. She is thankful. Knows now she'll go home alone. Doesn't want to let go. Touching the dying … touching the living … the dying's fading.*

Stewart turned away, hearing someone.

"Doctor, there's a sick baby in ER," Carla said, reappearing in the hospital room. "Can you come now?"

"Yes, soon as Dr. Gibon arrives." Stewart turned back to Sara, now stroking her husband's forehead.

*She's with him. I wasn't with dad.* "He'll be fine, Mrs. Colton." *Squeeze her hand … hate to pull away.*

Stewart hesitated. Sara said, "I'd rather be alone with him."

*Barry's breathing quietly now. Hardly breathing … seems so much better somehow. Slip his lids shut. Rest his eyes. No chance to shave. Looks unkempt … whiskers, clammy pale skin exuding sour scent, matted hair, mucous visible in his nose, drool sliding off the corner of his mouth. Wipe it … find something … the sheet. How can it matter to a dying man? Mrs. Colton doesn't mind. Dying at the end of summer's better than the middle of winter. Was for my dad. Winter's a cold death. This was really a warm death. Though he probably felt colder the more his pressure dropped. Maybe he didn't notice with the morphine.*

Sara seemed to breathe with Barry. She turned half her face to Stewart looking out the window, and said, "I called our children, but they live too far away to come this quick."

*Took us so long to relieve his suffering. Dad suffered too. My plea to his doctor for more morphine … sounded like asking a doctor's favor. Dad said it was fine … didn't want to bother anyone. Heroic—this saving life at any cost. Training … the right thing … no liability … no family emotions. Too busy to sit with them. Barry didn't suffer too long. Would've going to Houston. OR … the table … ICU … a bed like the table … the vent. Die alone … strange place … the last hour.*

Still staring out the window, Sara started when the oak leaves moved in the wind, and said to Stewart, "I wish we were home … but … we're here."

"Dr. Gibon. Thanks for coming." Stewart shook out the reverie then took the hand of the doctor who had guided them. He had a full head of gray hair, and was dressed in a white shirt, blue and burgundy striped tie, and charcoal sport coat. At 5:00 in the morning! He had posed the inevitable dilemma for the Coltons. How to act when the quality of your life hangs in balance with the quantity of your life. "In the crisis, Dr. Gibon, I tried to understand and follow your plan."

"Yes, Dr. Stewart," said Dr. Gibon, "We talked about it, but you carried it out."

"Sara, how are you?" said Dr. Gibon, bending down close to her face, hand on her shoulder. "I'm so sorry. Barry looks peaceful."

"Oh yes," said Sara. "Thank you for coming out in the middle of the night."

"Dr. Stewart, the baby," said Carla, reappearing. "It's crying."

"Yes. Right away." Stewart backed away from the bed, turning toward the door. While his eyes lingered on Sara and Dr. Gibon, left to complete their relationship with Barry, his heart felt the presence of his dad. ❖

**Tom Janisse, MD,** founded Peninhand Press in 1977, in Volcano, California, and has published: short stories—All Stories, All Kinds; California oral history—The Argonaut Mine Disaster; and poetry books—the volcano review 1-6, Peninhand, Falstaff Medical Poetry I and II, and Notes of a Cornerman. His published works include: a poem, "Dying Distant," in the *New England Journal of Medicine,* and a story, "Bring the Bottles," in the book *Emergency Room: Lives Saved and Lost: Doctors Tell Their Stories.* More information about Dr. Janisse can be found on page 104.

SPRING 2003

*soul of t*

**Christmas Face**
aluminum stylet sculpture
This sculpture was created from discarded endotracheal tubing and its aluminum stylet.

THESE SCULPTURES HELP ME REMEMBER THAT I AM TREATING PEOPLE, NOT SIMPLY BONES, JOINTS, OR X-RAYS.

**Faces #1**
aluminum stylet sculpture
This collection of faces is a hanging mobile and part of a series of sculptures created using anesthetic endotrachial tube stylets and industrial silicone glue. Dr. Bovill says that each of his sculptures represents a patient or colleague.

**David Bovill, MD,** is an orthopaedic surgeon at the Kaiser Permanente South Sacramento facility. He is involved with the American Academy of Orthopaedic Surgery traveling art show: Emotion Pictures (http://emotion.aaos.org/). His orthopaedic surgeon father and artist mother provide his inspiration. Dr. Bovill has worked in many media, including watercolors and oils. Currently, he prefers creating sculptures using discarded anesthetic endotracheal tube stylets, bending them into two- and three-dimensional faces. Find more about Dr. Bovill at: www.permanente.net/doctor/bovilld.

# Wuhao (Taki) Tu, MD

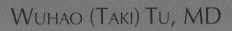

**Hillside**
oil

**Farmhouse**
oil

See page 9 for more
information about
**Wuhao (Taki) Tu, MD.**

*soul of t*

SUMMER 2003

*be healer*

# MITCHELL DANESH, MD

BY ABSTRACTING MY
PERCEPTION OF AN
AESTHETIC, I TRY TO
ACHIEVE AN EMOTIONAL
INTIMACY AND
PERCEPTION OF BEAUTY
WITH COLOR AND FORM.

**Green Woman**
acrylic on canvas
Dr. Danesh experiments
with color and form to
express abstracted beauty.

*soul of t*

**Camille Pissarro**
acrylic on canvas paper

**Mitchell Danesh, MD,** is the Regional Coordinating Chief of Neurology for Southern California, and is based in Woodland Hills, CA. His wife, Miki, is an artist and is his guide in this endeavor. Dr. Danesh's cover art was used in the Kaiser Permanente ad campaign during the 2004 Olympics and the "Camille Pissarro" portrait is cited in the French Internet encyclopedia: http://agora.qc.ca/mot.nsf/Dossiers/Pissarro.

I RECENTLY BEGAN SKETCHING AND PAINTING AND AM ESPECIALLY INTERESTED IN CONVEYING A PERSONAL EMOTIONAL LINK THROUGH THE PORTRAIT.

**Pierre-Auguste Renoir**
acrylic on canvas paper

143

# Anorexia: The Scream on the Other Side of Silence

*Why would one ever include autobiographical material about anorexia nervosa with articles on obesity? Many will be surprised that identical thought processes are often present in both: "Eating is the only thing left in my life that I can control."*

*Anorexia nervosa is still a condition of mystery and threat. Fifty years ago, serious physicians felt it was some yet-undetermined type of primary pituitary disorder. Now, physicians accept it as some yet-undetermined type of emotional disorder. Here we have the privilege and unusual opportunity to hear a woman describe her own thought processes—the method in her madness—during the course of several anorexic years. Surprisingly, most anorexic patients pass unnoticed through the offices of their physicians. We don't go out of our way to recognize that which we do not understand. And yet one wonders, disturbingly, how many patients might explain their problems clearly if we asked and listened?*

*— Vincent J Felitti, MD, Editor*

I invite you to starve with me. You will not like it at first, but ask yourself this: Did you like the first cigarette you smoked? The first whiskey that burned your throat? The first "one-night stand"? Each of those "fixes" helped you in some way, didn't it? It gave you the power to feel better—at least for a moment.

If you will join me, you will learn just how empowering starvation can be. You will be in complete control of yourself and of the people around you. How many people can say that and know that it is true?

Be me. A 13-year-old girl, 5'6" tall, about 120 lbs. Your mother is long since dead. Your father doesn't want you to live with him. You are now serving your sixth year of what feels like a life sentence with his sister and her husband. Your aunt—

"She"—sees everything about you as a reflection of herself. If your hair does not curl, there is not enough starch in your blouse, your tummy is not flat enough, your breasts not large enough, your shoes not polished enough, your smile not cheerful enough, then the neighbors will think She is not doing a good job. She makes you spend hours cleaning, ironing, weeding, and such; She even lines up paying jobs—and yet you must get As—That is important. It is a reflection on Her.

You like school. You love to learn. Every new thought inspires you. You are one of the brightest, most industrious, most compliant, and still popular girls in your class, yet She calls you "a goddam intellectual" when She is angry with you—and She is often angry. Nothing you do will ever be enough. You know it. Every mirror you look into reflects a person who will never be what She is supposed to be, no matter how hard She tries.

You cannot hide from the mirrors. They own you. Your aunt owns you. You will never be free. There is no escape ... or is there?

You begin to cut back on the already-meager portions She gives you. Did She notice? You think She did, but She hasn't said anything about it. Cut back more. What does the mirror say? Hmmm, still fat. Cut back more. A week goes by, a month, and now you are eating almost nothing, three or four bites of food a day, maybe a soft drink once in a while. Sometimes you cheat and eat the apple from your lunch before you throw it into the trash bin. You are SO HUNGRY ... ravenous, and yet you watch that brown paper sack leave your hand in freeze-frame slow motion, hear it THUD at the bottom of the bin, knowing its contents would stop the hunger. You will not eat. If you eat, you lose.

You're tired all the time now, but look! Your clothes fit loosely—finally! Progress.

> EVERY MIRROR YOU LOOK INTO REFLECTS A PERSON WHO WILL NEVER BE WHAT SHE IS SUPPOSED TO BE, NO MATTER HOW HARD SHE TRIES.

Your hunger is ravaging. You think of food all the time. The world takes on a clarity that you have never before noticed. You see every detail of every single thing. Sounds are louder, smells stronger. Another month goes by. You've lost 20 lbs. She notices! "Why aren't you eating? Are you sick?"

Oh yes, you're sick, but it is not the kind of sick that anyone can fix. You are on a mission to ensure that they cannot. You cannot let them get that close to you. If they do, they will hurt you. Oh yes, with hunger also comes fear—fear of absolutely everything. You're skittish. You jump at the slightest sound. You're wakeful, staring at the ceiling through the night. When you finally sleep, nightmares shatter your rest. There is no peace, but it is the price you pay for screaming the silent scream of starvation—the price you pay for power.

And it is worth the pricetag. She is now very disturbed by your weight loss—but not for the right reasons. Not because She loves you. Does anyone love you? She rages, "I spent hours sewing that for you, and now it doesn't fit you anymore!" VICTORY! Even your father notices. "Look at those arms! You'd better start eating. You look like a skeleton."

All you think about is food—the sight, the smell, what it used to taste like. It doesn't taste like anything anymore. Nothing tastes good to you. You've learned to replace hunger by imagining you've eaten. You feel the texture of mashed potatoes, sticking to the roof of your mouth. Your mental acuity seems to have sharpened—yet you have difficulty remembering. It is easy to slip into a trancelike state where you create your own reality—one in which She has no place.

In just a few months, you have mastered a most basic need: To eat. You are in control of your most essential self. In very little time, you have brought Her to her knees. She now begs you—begs you—to eat. She'll do anything to make you eat. You have total power. You have won.

You're almost 14 years old now and not a bad kid. You didn't really want to upset anyone—much—you just wanted to make it clear that you are upset. Had you said that, She'd have slapped you across the face, pulled your hair, given you a week of The Silent Treatment, and still more chores. Words failed you, so you drew them a picture: a stick figure of you.

Have they learned their lesson? Should you let them off the hook? Or should you make them really suffer, really sorry? Should you stop eating completely? You know what that means. You'll die. Should you die?

You're not a bad kid—not a stupid kid. Isn't this taking it a little too far? Okay, you caught the firefly—do you really need to kill it too? No, let the anger go. Forgive them. Forgive yourself for being so angry with them. Let yourself live. Let them have the power back again. You held it for a while—a long and painful while. Now you know you're stronger than they are. You know you can have the power back whenever you want it.

They were never trying to hurt you in the first place. ❖

*According to the National Institute of Mental Health, "Females are much more likely than males to develop an eating disorder … an estimated 0.5% to 3.7% of females suffer from anorexia and an estimated 1.1% to 4.2% suffer from bulimia … The mortality rate among people with anorexia has been estimated at 0.56% per year, or approximately 5.6% per decade, which is about 12 times higher than the annual death rate due to all causes of death among females ages 15 to 24 in the general population.[1]*

Reference
1. National Institute of Mental Health. The numbers count: mental disorders in America [Web page]. Available from: www.nimh.nih.gov/publicat/numbers.cfm (accessed July 22, 2003).

THE HUMERUS ZONE

Your problem is elementary, Mr. Holmes.
You're just a fictional Character.

THE HUMERUS ZONE

Doctor, I keep having this dream.
First, I dream I'm a tepee, then
I'm a wigwam. What does it mean?

The meaning of the dream is easy!
You must relax — you're just
two tents!

See page 91 for more
information about
**Don Wissusik, MA, MS.**

## To Alex at 3 a.m.

Demented baby, Daddy-held
Disoriented, labile mood, dysarthric cry

But behind clear eyes neurons myelinate
Donning long pants for the long day

Yet

All too soon neuronal antibodies find their prey
(You are your own worst enemy)
Aluminum and amyloid accumulate
Fibrils tangle

Dementia comes full spiral
A little old man cries in the night
And who will hold you then?

## Proposal

I am afraid of being poor
You fear the darker nights
I tense before a stranger's door
You're terrified of heights

I dread the ache of lonely days
You're timid in a crowd
I'm phobic of a barren phase
You shrink from seeming loud

I fear the future, you the now
I compliments, you jeers
I the why and you the how
Your anger and my tears

Thy fears make me protective
And mine may make you strong
Though singly we're defective
Combined, we'll get along.

More information about
**William Goldsmith, MD,**
can be found on page 99.

FALL 2003

*soul of t*

**Country Road**

photograph

This country road was
met on a relaxed drive
through rural Southern
California.

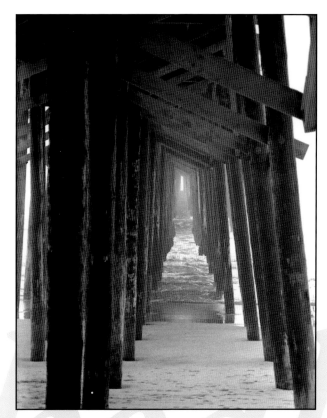

**Oceanside Pier**

photograph

The underside of
Oceanside Pier
reflects the
rhythmicity of
the ocean as the
waves crash
toward the shore.

For more information about
**Alan D Fremland, MD,** see
page 103.

# Why do you do, What you do, When you do, What you do

I'm getting older. I'm physically slower; my reflexes are not what they used to be. My eyes are worse, my hearing is diminished, my hair is graying, my joints ache sometimes, and I'm not as quick or precise at remembering as I once was. As great as the gradual changes in my physical performance are, my personality changes are perhaps more significant. My type A, aggressive personality has mellowed. Time has been a great teacher. Experience has been a great teacher. Success and failure have taught invaluable lessons.

Once quick to argue, firm in my intellectual stances and convinced of the correctness of my position, I'm different. After overwhelming others with "forceful" arguments and later being proven wrong, "I know that I don't know what I know." "Today's truth is tomorrow's error," is a mantra. Tolerance of other viewpoints and intellectual stances has evolved. Having made many thoughtless or careless mistakes myself, the willingness to forgive has appeared. I try to lead by facilitation. One doesn't need to have the answers as leader; but one must allow them to come from others. Even when a solution seems obvious, it's good to let someone else suggest it. When solutions come from the group rather than from the leader, the solutions are more readily accepted.

Having the brightest light in the fixture may unbalance the total illumination. Historically impatient, a certain phlegmatism has evolved in me. Suppressing colleagues when chairing a meeting causes serious conscious and subconscious resentment. Once quick to rush to combat, I pick the battles that can be won, avoiding the battles that will inevitably be lost. The wisdom of the "win-win" scenario seems powerful. When you create a loser, you fertilize the field of revolution. Sharing victory encourages the growth of comradeship. Somehow the "team triumph" seems to produce longer-lasting joy than the individual achievement. Whatever team I have been associated with, the successes always seem to live on in the members.

My youth's compulsion to always be right has morphed to the acceptance of personal fallibility. I am quick to apologize. Although cavalry Captain Nathan Brittles in a John Wayne movie[1] said "Never apologize, Mister. It's a sign of weakness!" I don't ascribe to that belief.

Though capable of inflicting pain, I do so most often inadvertently. When guilty, I apologize profusely and sincerely and try to make amends. Earlier in life, I lacked the courage to be wrong or to admit the error. There was fear that either would diminish me. Time and pain have corrected that misconception.

Without wishing it, there is less sensitivity to others' feelings than I might desire. I've learned to compensate by observation but understand that observation is a poor substitute for true empathy. Having become more sensitive to my own failings, I am better able to see when I'm tiresome to others. I've seen my arrival put disappointment on faces. This has made me willing to walk away rather than to inflict myself on others.

I am quick with a compliment when it is deserved. I am slower to criticize, perhaps not as slow as I should be but better than I once was. After a leadership course, I spent a lot of time distributing compliments to colleagues. This was met with suspicion. I persevered. What once was met with mistrust is now met with appreciation.

I've learned to value friends and to mourn the acquisition of enemies. It is said that one can never have enough friends but that one enemy is too many. I adhere to that belief, though I remain too adept at antagonizing others and producing animus.

Patience has evolved. I have learned to plant the seeds of progress and fertilize them for years until they are ready to germinate and grow. Sometimes when they grow, no one remembers who did the planting. This omission no longer bothers me, as the fruit of the progress feeds my hunger for recognition. I accept both compliments and criticism with grace. Both once embarrassed me, but that too has passed with advancing time.

I've learned the value of communication. Missed communication, late communication, inaccurate communication—these are root causes of many of the problems we face daily. The ability to communicate truth and to avoid communicating untruth must be constantly regenerated. We are constantly tempted by the power of the lie. It is like the "power of the dark side." I am as prone to "spin a tale" as the next person, but generally succumb reluctantly and with remorse afterward.

All these things and more contribute to my behavior. My personal evolution is a daily ebb and flow of experience.

Why do I do what I do when I do what I do? I do what I do when I do what I do, because I am still learning. ❖

Reference
1. She Wore a Yellow Ribbon. RKO/Warner Bros Video 1949.

**Calvin Weisberger, MD,** is Regional Coordinating Chief of Cardiology for the Southern California Permanente Medical Group, and Chairman of the Regional Product Council. He is co-author of the book Practical Nuclear Cardiology. He has written other pieces in various venues.

**The "Three Redheaded" Sisters**
watercolor

MY INSPIRATION
COMES FROM MY
LIFE EXPERIENCES
AND TRAVELS.

**"Honu" has the
Right of Way**
watercolor

**Patty Stelz, RN,** works in the
Emergency Department at the
Kaiser Permanente Sunnyside
Medical Center in Portland, OR.
She is a mostly self-taught artist
and works primarily in watercolor.

# Index of Contributors

CPMG: Colorado Permanente Medical Group; GHP: Group Health Permanente; MAPMG: Mid-Atlantic Permanente Medical Group; NWP: Northwest Permanente; PMGMA*: Permanente Medical Group of Mid-America; SCPMG: Southern California Permanente Medical Group; TCPMG*: The Carolina Permanente Medical Group; TPMG: The Permanente Medical Group.
*No longer a Permanente Medical Group.